Journeys in
Community

Journeys in
Community

Father-daughter conversations
about faith, love, doubt and hope

John Harvey and Ruth Harvey

wild goose
publications www.**ionabooks**.com

Contents

Foreword

Journeys in Community is grounded in stories. John and Ruth Harvey, father and daughter, both ordained, both storytellers, root us in the ordinary and offer prayers, liturgies, stories, reflections and language to meet the heart. The richness of this writing lies in the trustability of the lives from which it's come. These are not prayers based on moody, misty imaginations of a disembodied Celtic spirituality. They are prayers to help you survive moody, misty complexities in modern Scotland and beyond. It's the kind of writing to turn to in moments when you're feeling lost. This book will welcome you home, with justice, courage, humour and delight.

Pádraig Ó Tuama, former Leader of the Corrymeela Community

*This book is dedicated to
the members and staff of the Iona Community
and all royalties will be donated
to support the youth work of the community.*

Introduction (John and Ruth)

Leader: How good and how lovely it is
All: To live together in community.

These words, part of the morning service in Iona Abbey, resonate deeply for any who have lived together in community. Yes, indeed, it can be *'good and lovely'* to share deeply and dream widely with others in community, to share the 'common life' of eating, sleeping, washing, cleaning, praying and working that is formed in intentional community. It is also hard work, exhausting and for some may even be painful to live together in this way – where the challenge of finding space alone in the midst of noise can be overwhelming, and the relentless effort of engaging with others seems to leave little space for growth.

Spending an intense 10 years in intentional community as a family, we grew together, children and adults, in a unique way: John in his early ministry, with Molly, as part of the Gorbals Group Ministry, then as part of the newly formed Resident Group on Iona; Ruth as their child, born in Gorbals, and moving with John, Molly and her siblings to Iona aged 5.

And perhaps in community we also grew apart in tender ways not easy to articulate: saw the spaces between us in the forming and re-forming of communal life on a weekly basis in Glasgow and in Iona Abbey, which we were both privileged to share.

Here then we offer reflections on the outworking of part of our shared spiritual journey, honed over years of father-daughter conversation and sharing. We don't pretend to offer reflections on behalf of our wider family – that would be a whole other work. Instead, we simply offer thoughts, reflections and meditations focused around parts of the Christian year that have been formative to both of us, and looked at through the lens of life in intentional community.

The book has five chapters. Chapter one shares some reflections on how each of us became caught up in the story and the life of the Iona Community, both on Iona and on the mainland. There then follow four chapters of reflections and prayers centred on the main seasons of the Christian year, with an introduction to each one.

Late-night conversations about the existence of God and the power of the psalms; walks along Argyll tracks sharing dreams of vocation and calling and wondering about 'God's call'; raucous singing in the family car when liberation songs from South Africa hit our cassette player; mighty meals around the kitchen table with talk of faith, love, politics, sexuality, prayer, church and the Iona Community; railing against a sense of 'thrown-ness', when it becomes apparent that you've landed in a time and space in the world not of your choosing and asking: what happened to land us in this Presbyterian, ecumenical context? These are just some of the memories we recalled as part of our shared family life, growing and deepening together as father and daughter, in a wider extended family of faiths and doubts.

Because living together in community is not always '*good and lovely*' (it has brought its share of pain as well as joy), reflections of grief, lament, conflict and despair therefore also weave their pattern through our shared journey, finding resonance in the tenderness of human relationships, and in the gritty reality of stories of faith.

Growing up together in this context we have continued to talk about faith, doubt, love, loss and the existence of God. And we have sought in our professional lives to find expression of these conversations in private contemplation, in family life, in public worship, in work for peace and justice, and in the intentional Christian community that remains our shared context: the Iona Community.

We hope that this collection will augment other conversations on faith, love, doubt and hope.

John: 'Now in my ninth decade, perhaps slightly to my surprise, I am nonetheless finding that it's very life-giving to go back over some reflections from my earlier ministry, and journey through them with Ruth, seeing them in a new light and gaining new insight from our shared conversations. It is also very challenging to read these earlier writings towards the end of my life, and find that while they still push me on and call me out, they also speak very urgently to my inner journey, which has, faith tells us, no end.'

Ruth: 'In the midst of busyness, it can be easy to become lost in minutiae – and so I continue to seek out those people and places that ground me, root me, remind me of the bigger picture to which I belong. Talking with Dad has always been one of these experiences. Being reminded of the stages on the journey of faith, not only through a calendar, or liturgical year, but also through the seasons of life, puts all that is in front of me today into perspective, and draws me simultaneously out of myself, while also giving me permission to dwell in the stillness that is within.'

– John Harvey and Ruth Harvey

On life in Community

My journey to the Iona Community (John)

My journey to the Iona Community started, like many people's, first with meeting Iona Abbey, and only then the Community. The two events, however, happened virtually simultaneously and all within the space of three months, over the spring and early summer of 1958 as I turned 21, and had, for me, the force of a Damascus Road conversion. And if that sounds dramatic, all I can say is that's exactly how it felt!

It began, as many similar journeys did in those days, with George MacLeod. He came, as Moderator of the General Assembly and a former distinguished member of the Regiment, as the guest of honour to a dinner held by the 1st Battalion of the Argyll and Sutherland Highlanders, where I was then serving as a National Service 2nd Lieutenant. The Chaplain knew I was thinking of 'going in for the ministry' and introduced me to the great man. George, always on the look out for potential recruits to his still fairly young Community, gave me his card and told me to phone him when I got out. Flattered, of course, at being at the receiving end of such attention, I called him – and he stood me to lunch in Glasgow. The outcome was that he arranged for me to go to Iona for three months to, as he rather vaguely put it, 'help us to build a road'.

At this point in my life, I may have heard of Iona, but never of the Iona Community. My faith journey up till then had led me from a pretty traditional middle-class church background, through a youthful evangelical conversion experience, followed by a sharp rejection of all things religious (mainly because I felt I was being offered answers to questions that I wasn't actually asking), back to a vague desire to study theology and explore the possibility of ministry, largely through the influence of the Army Chaplain who introduced me to MacLeod in the first place. My knowledge of Scottish church history was virtually nil – I often say that at that time I think I assumed that the church first appeared in Scotland around about the middle of the 16th century, with John Knox.

Landing on Iona in May 1958, where no one expected me, because George had forgotten to tell anyone I was coming (and where the building of a road was never mentioned), felt like what I imagine Neil Armstrong may have felt like when he landed on the moon. Everything was new. The journey itself was new – by train to Oban, finding the boat to Mull, being landed on the old Craignure pier by small boat (no car ferries in those days), rattling across Mull in an ancient Bowmans bus, and then tossing across the Sound in the launch that served as the Iona ferry, crewed by ferrymen Dan and Angie. Walking up to the Abbey (be-kilted, with my stuff in an army knapsack), I stared in amazement at the ruins of the Nunnery, and the Relig Odhrain, and then at the totally unexpected sight of the Abbey, squatting there, as someone has described it, *'like a Gothic dwarf'* in the evening sun.

The morning of my first full day on Iona, I came down the night stairs into the north transept for the morning service, in a sort of daze. Ahead of me, the small group of masons and carpenters who were working that year on the rebuilding of the cloisters had already gathered in the choir stalls. I was astounded by the view, from the stairs, of the south transept, the Argyll Tomb, the arches of the south choir aisle – ever since, this has been my favourite view of the Church. The service was a revelation – ordinary working men, in their working clothes, saying the responses, singing the hymns, kneeling for prayer – I'd never seen anything like it, never experienced a service of this nature in my life. And then out they went, straight to their work in the cloisters – leaving me sitting there, trying to take it all in.

From that day to this, sentimental as it must sound, I've felt entangled in what I can only call a love affair with that building and its story. Over the decades I've worked in it – as a guide, in the shop, as a new member of the Community working on the building of the west range, as the Warden, as the Leader of the Community – I've lived in it, struggled with its staffing, with its upkeep, with its refurbishment, with its foibles and its peculiarities, I've laughed and loved and cried in it, and of course I have worshipped in it, as a participant and as a leader of worship, more times than I can count. My heart still lifts every time I see it, and I thank God for the tens of thousands who have ensured it still stands, and still inspires millions from all around the world, the faithful and the doubters and the seekers after God, however they conceive God to be.

Meeting the Iona Community happened in stages over that spring and early summer. It really began in Camas, the Community's outdoor centre on nearby Mull. Ralph Morton, the Deputy Leader of the Community who was in charge on Iona at that time (George was abroad), asked me after a few weeks to stand in as cook in Camas – probably the role in life for which I was, and still am, the most unsuited! There I met and lived for three weeks with young people from disadvantaged urban areas and from institutions, and watched as the place worked its magic. I began to glimpse something of the purpose of the Community: its care for young people, its commitment to walk with people on the margins, and the way in which the worship of the Community, expressed in Camas in the wonderful Chapel of the Nets, or out of doors beside the fishing boats, could begin to make sense to unchurched people, on a daily basis, in the place of the common life. And things began to click, too, for me.

A few weeks later, that year's new members began to arrive on Iona. I can't remember now who all of them were – but they made a powerful impression, with their leading of services, their intense discussions, which I sometimes was able to overhear, and their activity in the rebuilding work every day. They were, I think, all ministers, mainly from Scotland, but I do remember one from the USA. And I was able to watch George MacLeod, back from abroad, relate to them, chivvy them on, argue with them, challenge them – and of course involve them in much of what was going on in the island. And most memorably, I was privileged to be led in worship by George MacLeod himself – an experience which all who have shared, never, ever forget.

Memories of that first three months on Iona abound. The Dartmouth Royal Naval cadets throwing stones out of their hut windows all night to try to silence the corncrakes. Dancing the Highland fling on a table in the refectory to the pipes of Calum MacPherson, Master Carpenter and Foreman of the rebuilding. Guiding a group from a National Trust cruise ship round the Abbey, with a guidebook in one hand to keep me right – most of them probably already knew far more than I could ever tell them about Columba and his mission in the sixth century. Offering to take two visiting Australian deaconesses to the Marble Quarry after having been there only once myself (on a pilgrimage led by Johnny MacMillan, one of the very early craftsmen from Govan) – they never saw the Marble Quarry yet!

At the end of my three months, I left, with great reluctance, to get ready to go to university. George MacLeod, with his impassioned commitment to non-violence as the heart of the Gospel, had already convinced me to resign my National Service Commission and return to the ranks as a Territorial Army private – not that the Army paid much attention! But my main thought, as I got onto the wee ferry to head for Craignure, Oban and then Glasgow, was – *I hope I can return, and I hope I can hold on to the new vision of the Christian faith that I have been given* – a faith for every day of the week, a faith which saw work and worship as two sides of the same coin, a faith which called for active involvement in the whole life of the whole world. Over the decades, with the help of the Iona Community, of course what has happened is that, more often despite myself than because of anything in me, that faith has held on to *me* – and it holds me still.

At this point, I need to be very clear. For me, the Iona Community as a movement has always been rooted both on Iona and on the mainland. Clearly the Abbey, with all its many resonances in my journey, has been central – but only if taken in conjunction with what my membership of the Community, renewed as we all must do year after year, has meant for my life. I firmly believe, as George MacLeod wrote in one of his great prayers, that 'We are Your temple not made with hands. We are Your body. If every wall should crumble, and every church decay, we are Your habitation ... It is not just the interior of these walls: it is our own inner beings You have renewed.'

Two of the most challenging, and fulfilling, periods of my faith journey, inspired by the Iona Community, took place outside the walls, both material and institutional, of the Church of Scotland.

For eight years, from 1963 to 1971, Molly and I were part of the Gorbals Group Ministry in inner-city Glasgow. I have written elsewhere about this experiment in urban mission (*Bridging the Gap: Has the Church Failed the Poor?*, St Andrew Press, 1987), and Ron Ferguson, my predecessor as Leader of the Community, has explored it more extensively in *Geoff: The Life of Geoffrey M Shaw* (Famedram, 1979). This was an attempt by a small group of ministers, social workers, teachers and others to follow the example of the early church, as described in the Book of Acts, by sharing all things in common and living alongside families in poverty as a witness to the values of the Gospel, without the support of the institutional church.

Towards the end of my active ministry I spent five years with the Craighead Institute, an ecumenical, Ignatian-inspired body committed to working alongside congregations and parishes seeking to develop a more integrated, active Christian witness in their local communities. With the Institute, I helped lead weekend workshops with Christians of different denominations in the West of Scotland; I travelled frequently to war-torn Croatia, just at the end of the terrible civil war in that region, to help groups seek ways to reconciliation and to find new expressions of their faith; I was sent on regular visits to Lithuania, to help Christians there work out how to live in a society recently liberated from the straightjacket of Soviet dominance. There they told us, '*We learnt to think with two heads – one to think what we really thought, the other to think what the regime told us to think.*' I was also asked to work with Roman Catholic religious orders as they struggled with their communal life and obedience – and came to admire so much of the commitment and radical discipleship I so often met there.

Choices

When Molly and I married in 1963 we chose to start our life together as part of the Gorbals Group Ministry in inner-city Glasgow. For us, as a newly married couple, it was an intense and exhilarating – as well as hugely challenging – time. It was a choice. We were always clear that, unlike most of our neighbours, we could choose to leave at any time. It was not a choice that our parents found easy to understand – and it was made much more difficult for them when our children started to be born.

Children have no choice, of course, as to where and into what context they are born. But in choosing to live in Gorbals, and have our first three children born there, we made that choice on their behalf. Looking back, we're ambivalent, to say the least, about the wisdom of the choice we made. We have since had the opportunity to talk with other parents, and other children, who have lived with the consequences of such choices, and who have helped us to face them ourselves. It's a humbling and precious experience to listen to our own children speaking of these consequences as well – the good, and the bad.

Perhaps the greatest challenge arising from the choices we made, both in having children in the context of a community living in a crumbling Victorian slum, and then bringing them to live in another community on a remote Hebridean island, lay in the shock we all felt when we found ourselves living as a nuclear family on the mainland in 1976.

But in and through all these choices, and their consequences, the learning curve, certainly for Molly and myself, and hopefully for our children too, has been a stretching and a deepening of what it means to be human in an interdependent world, and to be children of 'God', however we and they understand that elusive word.

For my swansong in paid employment, I worked for the Church of Scotland again, this time as an Interim Minister. I was asked to work with three different congregations for short periods each time (the longest for two years), all of whom were going through times of difficulty in their institutional lives. My time in Gorbals, with the Iona Community, and with the Craighead Institute, all helped me to understand, and hopefully to assist, these congregations – and it was a privilege to share in their struggles, and to see, close up, how much commitment ordinary church members were willing to put into the life and work of the church.

In retirement Molly and I have found great inspiration in sharing in the establishment and development of the first Poverty Truth Commission (PTC) in the UK here in Glasgow. The PTC brings the real experts in poverty, those who have had to live in and with it for their whole lives, together with those who have the power to affect and change it – people in politics, in the media, in business, in education, in the caring professions. The PTC then accompanies them in making a difference through listening to, and working closely with, each other, instead of speaking across one another and entering into the blame game.

Being a Child of God in Community: Iona 1975 (Ruth)

Hands held tightly across the row of six bodies, bent bold against the gale, we are gripped close by our teacher as we stride home through the wild wind. She stops at MacLean's Cross. 'Look!' she says, peering through the murk across the Sound of Iona. 'Look! The waterfall on Mull is being blown upwards!'

And it surely was – powering water, pouring up.

For the first 10 years of my life I lived in intentional Christian communities, the last five of these as part of the Resident Group in Iona Abbey. We were there as a family. But where most of my contemporaries lived with a small group of relatives in a house, and went to school with many more children, our lives were lived back to front. We lived with up to 50 folk in a restored Benedictine Abbey, and I attended a school of five pupils – the majority of whom were my relatives.

That blustery winter morning in 1975 we were no Celtic poets scribbling reflections to God's glory in the margins of our journals, as the holy men on our island home had been some 1300 years earlier. But we were just as awestruck by divine power and passion as the rain streamed down our faces, and 'up' the cliffs of Mull.

Few unrelated playmates meant we fell back on inner resources. The wildness of the barn and the beach became our playground, the feral foraging along the seashore our play. I remember a glorious evening as an eight-year-old spent alone by the jetty, getting first the hems, then the knees and then the waist of my trousers wet. I kept going, up to my chest, my chin in the Atlantic, until I was part of the ocean, fully clad, fully alone, up to my neck in creation. An Ezekiel moment of both awe and terror.

The island of Iona is a sliver of beauty: windswept, holy Atlantic gneiss and granite. Yet as children we knew little about the geology, never mind the spirituality of the island.

We had arrived from the Gorbals in 1971, fresh from inner-city Glasgow, where our large Victorian tenement home, along with hundreds of others left to rot in the late 19th century, was now being razed to the ground, to be replaced by prefabricated skyscrapers that would last no more than three decades. The people's lives were turned upside down. 'Decanted', they called it, from their homes to 'streets on end', whole communities were 'diasporated'. Our decanting, to Iona, was a different kind of culture shock – the first few weeks my sister and I held hands tightly to cross the village street, anxious to follow the Green Cross Code, puzzled by the lack of zebra crossings to protect us from the two cars that passed daily.

Our parents, Molly and John, had been part of the pioneering Gorbals Group Ministry, modelled on the East Harlem Protestant Parish of 1960s New York, where groups of Christians committed to the social gospel chose to live alongside the poor – sharing money, food, prayer and work in common, committed to lifting hearts and bodies out of poverty. The demolition of our home meant we moved to be part of the Iona Community – a similarly prophetic group of Christians committed to peace and justice and the non-violent transformation of the world.

For me, as an extroverted child, this was a glorious way to grow up! I relished the common space, the Abbey Church worship twice daily, the shared meals with 50, the freedom of the island. I assumed that what we had was the norm.

Small wonder, then, that the reality check of being 'decanted' from there, first to a tiny cottage in the middle of nowhere, then to a housing estate in central Scotland where sectarianism was rife – and where to admit your religious allegiance could result in being spat on or worse – was a shock. Not as big a shock, however, as having to learn to live in a home with only six, and to go to school with hundreds.

The resilience of children to weather the storms not just of our Atlantic weather system, but of adult choice, is awesome. The damage we can do to children, inadvertently, in our well-intentioned adult decision-making requires careful reflection. As I continue to 'decant' my life daily, from experience to experience, I live in equal awe of those children whose lives are propelled into situations of emotional or physical danger through no choice of their own, and whose resilience in the face of war, hunger, terror and death knows no bounds.

Triple-belonging: Cumbria 2019

Years later, when my husband Nick and I decided that our joint spiritual belonging, with our children, was to the Society of Friends (Quakers), I made an adult commitment to belong more fully – and have since described my triple-belonging as three essential legs of a stool. I dwell in my Presbyterian heritage because it is my inheritance – and like all such inheritances, I belong to my church with comfort and discomfort in equal measure. I dwell in my Quaker belonging because it's one way that my now-family can hand-on-heart attend weekly worship and all feel at home. But I live through my Iona Community belonging because it reminds me that while I may be a member of three human institutions, my true belonging is to a greater, wider, deeper community of worldwide believers of all hues and traditions.

Advent and Christmas

Introduction (John and Ruth)

Advent and Christmas are all about incarnation, and the mystery of the whole season. John can date that feeling back to his early childhood, and the first watch night service he was taken to, at the age of seven. Apart from the thrill of being allowed up – and out! – so late, he still remembers the atmosphere of the service – no long sermon, quiet, reflective, and the mystery of God becoming a human being. Until then he had experienced the story of Christmas on a very horizontal level – presents, parties, food. It was then that he became aware of the vertical level of the story.

Fast-forward to the Christmas house parties he was responsible for running in the Abbey in the early 1970s, where the mystery was the main thrust of the story as the programme developed. There was the quietness, the waiting, the expectation – the sheer size of the story as well, opening up everyone to a new experience of God – so huge, and yet so personal.

'Mystery' is sometimes confused with 'magic'. George Mackay Brown, the great Orcadian poet, once wrote: *'Transfigured by ceremony, the truths we could not otherwise endure come to us.'*[1] Mystery – and ceremony – are surely the right words to use about this season, emphasising that we are never in control of God – God cannot be manipulated. In the Gospel narrative, a very powerful emphasis is placed on this by the fact that it is the angel Gabriel who brings Mary the news that she is to be the mother of Jesus. In Hebrew angelology, Gabriel is normally the messenger of doom. Small wonder, then, that Mary is terrified when he appears! It was the Jewish Holocaust survivor Elie Wiesel who wrote: *'Whenever an angel says: "Be not afraid!" you'd better start worrying. A big assignment is on the way.'*[2] True – but along with the big assignment comes the big promise, that *'nothing will be impossible with God'*. It's missing the point to ask 'how did it happen?'. That's a distraction, trying to explore the viability or otherwise of angels and virgin births. The point is: there's something immense and mysterious on the cards here, and we should be prepared.

Ruth's early memories of Christmas at the Abbey are of humour and delight. She recalls the Christmas house parties as a chance to celebrate with other families, and being part of the Christmas plays. *The Shepherds' Story*, for example, in the refectory, where the servery was the changing room, and the route through the kitchen to the cloisters, and back up the refectory stairs, meant that we could 'surprise' our audience. Health and safety would have something to say now about mini shepherds dashing, crooks in hand, through a working kitchen. And the play *Michael Mouse*, a story of the mystery being made real from the perspective of the outsiders, the little people.

Then, growing up on the mainland, she remembers the clash of cultures: being a teenager in the 1980s while at the same time being a member of a church family. Shortly after leaving Iona, she and her siblings made homemade Christmas cards to give to their new school friends, only to have them returned as not acceptable – their friends expected 'real' ones!

Worshipping as a Quaker, while Ruth can sometimes feel bereft of a liturgical focus, she rejoices in the celebration of each moment as sacramental, and the mystery of Christmas, somehow, unfolding each day, without it ever becoming mundane.

In her Iona Community Family Group, they share an ALTER-nativity meal at the start of Advent (www.alternativity.org.uk). This simple meal, with table laid to include a symbolic empty place for John the Baptist, for Mary, for Jesus, and for the world's poor, reminds them of the mystery, of the simplicity of the story, in the global context of the hunger and poverty in which we all live – but also of the hope that the season brings.

Approaching Advent

Gathering at Advent: A prayer of approach,
and some thoughts (John)

It's good,
Living God,
to gather again at Advent
and hear the glad sounds
of the coming Christ.

The words of faith
in scripture and in song
gladden our hearts
and challenge our consciences
once again.

And it's good
to take time to listen
to Advent sounds
amidst the din of Christmas
that can so deafen us
every year.

So we thank you
for this time of listening
and of waiting
and of reflecting –
we seek the help
of the Holy Spirit
to use this time well.

Living God,
we know there are other sounds

that we need to hear at Advent.
So forgive us
when we do not hear
the sounds of our sisters and brothers
across the world
in refugee camp and disaster zone;
when we do not hear
the sounds of the suffering earth,
of dying species, of polluted seas;
when we do not hear
the sounds of our lonely neighbour,
of broken families,
of empty homes.

Help us, by your grace,
not to let Advent sweep us
mindlessly towards the birthday
of Jesus.

May the sounds of our faith
inspire and encourage us
to reflection, to action, to love;
and may this time
be one
not of nostalgia
so much as of preparation –
a time for us
to help prepare the way of the Lord
now, in our world.
We pray in Jesus' name. Amen

December 6, 2009, Iona Parish Church

Advent is above all a time of waiting, and of mystery. This anonymous reflection, from the 15th century, captures that sense well:

> *Thou shalt know Christ when he comes*
> *Not by any din of drums,*
> *Nor by the vantage of his airs,*
> *Nor by anything he wears,*
> *Neither by his crown nor his gown –*
> *But his presence known shall be*
> *In the holy harmony*
> *That his coming makes in thee.*

In a similar vein, words by Emily Dickinson offer a wise observation, which we preachers especially need to learn, over and over again:

> *Tell all the truth but tell it slant -*
> *Success in Circuit lies*
> *Too bright for our infirm Delight*
> *The Truth's superb surprise*
> *As Lightning to the Children eased*
> *With explanation kind*
> *The Truth must dazzle gradually*
> *Or every man be blind -*[3]

'*The Truth must dazzle gradually*'! Not just a recommendation as to how to grasp, or rather be grasped by, the Truth, but surely a statement of what actually happens in real life? Yes, one can be struck all of a sudden by a 'Damascus Road' experience – but to actually be drawn into anything like the fullness of the Truth, that takes time – loads of it – a lifetime, and beyond.

The Advent table is set: An ALTERnativity meal (Ruth)

Soon our kitchen will be filled with friends, and strangers, gathered for an Advent meal. We will worship, eat, laugh and pray. Our food will be simple: we will share soup, oatcakes, baked potatoes, cheese and chocolate. It will be fair trade or locally sourced. We will drink milk and water, because that's all we need. We will sit side by side: young and old, friend and stranger. And we will celebrate together the joy of waiting for the birth of Christ.

We will have places laid for each person joining us. And we will keep one place empty, as a symbol of the person who is the focus of our waiting this Advent: Jesus.

We will think about some of the people of Advent – of Mary, waiting as a single mother to give birth; of John, waiting in the wilderness. And we'll think about ourselves, waiting as if this was the first Christmas, not knowing exactly what is going to happen, but expectant, sure that something earth-shattering is on the cards.

As we enter this time of Advent, of waiting, it's hard to put the brakes on Christmas: how many more online shopping days? How soon can we put up the decorations? When can we start eating mince pies? In our headlong rush, let's remember the gift of patience, of waiting. And let's rekindle an impatience on behalf of those who should not have to wait: refugees waiting for shelter; children of Damascus, of all conflict, waiting for fighting to stop; the kidnapped waiting to be released; the hungry waiting for food.

Who are the people around you who are waiting for love, for justice this Christmas? ...

Advent waiting: A reflection and prayer (Ruth)

See, the former things have come to pass,
and new things I now declare ...

Isaiah 42:9 (NRSV)

But Jesus looked at them and said: 'For mortals it is impossible,
but for God all things are possible.'

Matthew 19:26 (NRSV)

He said: 'Abba, Father, for you all things are possible ...'

Mark 14:36 (NRSV)

For the generations who have grown up with the Internet, the smartphone, space travel and the mapping of the human genome, it's tempting to imagine that all things are possible. Surely one day soon we'll end all wars, cure cancer, reverse climate change, feed the world.

That these things are actually possible – that the human race has the knowledge and the power to make these things come to pass – is not in doubt. What is in doubt is the will to make them happen.

The good news of Advent is that God makes all things new – and all things possible – by 'birthing' in the heart of humanity. God does this by inviting us first to reflect on *'the former things that have come to pass'* – by asking us to view, through the eyes of faith, God's own track record, and then act accordingly.

For what has God already done? Created the universe out of nothing. Breathed life into mortals. Planted within us the knowledge of God and goodness *'more deeply than all that is wrong'* (from an Iona Community affirmation). Shown us that we are made to live not alone but in community. Made clear what God requires of us – to do justice, to love kindness and to walk humbly with God.

All this God has already done. Now let us open our hearts and our arms to each other, to tear down the walls of force and of fear that separate us, and to work with God to *make all things new*.

Living God,
your ways are indeed not our ways,
nor your thoughts our thoughts.

We look back
with pride in what we have achieved;
you ask us to look back
in wonder at what you have done.

We look forward,
conscious of our need,
and cautiously confident in ourselves;
you ask us to look forward,
to know your will for all creation
and to put our trust in you.

But most of all, this Advent, we pray:
give us the grace to live in the present moment;
to welcome your coming in Jesus,
and to attend to what we must now do.
So may our impossibilities
become your possibilities,
in the new things that you will bring to birth
in our world.
We pray in Jesus' name.
Amen

Songs of deliverance: Working with the Psalms and John's
Gospel in Advent (Ruth)

This series of seven prayers, originally written for 'Sanctuary First',
forms a pattern for reflection for the first week of December,
beginning with World AIDS Day. The prayers and reflections,
focusing on the notion of deliverance, delve into some of the pain,
confusion and despair of loss, conflict, war, rage and pain in the
world. In and through all, they attempt to weave hope, through
words of prayer inspired by the Psalms and words from the Gospel
of John.

Songs of deliverance, 1st December: World AIDS Day

Song (based on Psalm 13):

How long, O Lord,
will you quite forget me?
How long, O Lord,
will you turn your face from me?
How long, O Lord,
must I suffer in my soul?
How long, how long,
O Lord?

(From *Heaven Shall Not Wait* and *When Grief Is Raw*, John L. Bell and
Graham Maule) [4]

Reading: Psalm 13:1–6

Prayer:

Compassionate God,
walk with us who live with HIV or AIDS;

weep with us who live with Ebola or other incurable diseases;
keen and wail with us who grieve over a loved one gone;
and lest we forget, turn our face,
or walk on the other side of the road;
disturb, cajole and transform us
who would rather forget all who suffer.
Amen

Songs of deliverance, 2nd December: Courage to love

Song (based on Psalm 13):

How long, O Lord,
must this grief possess my heart?
How long, O Lord,
must I languish night and day?
How long, O Lord,
shall my enemy oppress?
How long, how long,
O Lord?

(From *Heaven Shall Not Wait* and *When Grief Is Raw*, John L. Bell and
Graham Maule)

Reading: Psalm 77:7–13

Prayer:

Courageous God,
walk with us who live with war, or the threat of war;
weep with us whose children wake in terror in the night,
scared of bullets, petrified by pain,
afraid to the core of a grim death;
keen and wail with us who grieve over each human heart

shattered, destroyed, torn apart, stopped in the grip of war;
rage with us over visions trampled, dreams destroyed.

And then, dear Lord, still our racing souls;
bring us back to the deep, impatient,
courageous love
which overcomes all fear.
Amen

Songs of deliverance, 3rd December: Trust in the face of danger

Song (based on Psalm 13):

Look now, look now, and answer me, my God.
Give light, give light, lest I sleep the sleep of death.
Lest my enemies rejoice at my downfall,
look now, look now, O Lord.

(From *Heaven Shall Not Wait* and *When Grief Is Raw*, John L. Bell and
Graham Maule)

Reading: Psalm 140:1–8

Prayer:

In the face of mortal danger, pain and anguish,
God of in-sight – lighten the inner path
    of love and compassion in each of us
    to bring love from the inside out,
    lest we sleep the sleep of death
    and turn our backs on ourselves
    and you, the very source of transformation.

God of out-sight – lighten the outer path
    of justice and peace in each of us,

in our communities,
our places of worship,
our world,
lest we sleep the sleep of death
and turn our backs on those who suffer.

God of light: give hope, give courage, give peace.
Amen

Songs of deliverance, 4th December: Will someone listen now,
please? …

Song (based on Psalm 6):

Hear me, Lord, and draw near;
in mercy, listen to my plea:
I am worn out, weary and exhausted,
and my soul is troubled deep within me.

(From *Psalms of Patience, Protest and Praise* and *Love from Below,* John
L. Bell and Graham Maule)[5]

Reading: John 1:40–45

Prayer:

Hear me, Lord, and draw near:
I am poor, my children are hungry,
I am in debt, there is no money for Christmas …

Silence

Hear me, Lord, and draw near:
I am rich, I have overspent,

my greed has overcome me and I no longer know
the difference between need and want ...

Silence

Hear me, Lord, and draw near:
hospital is my only salvation;
I am worn out, exhausted and troubled by illness
in body, mind and spirit ...

Silence

And as we cry for help,
may we also hear you cry to us:
'Come, follow me, and I will give you rest.'
Amen

*Songs of deliverance, 5th December: Will someone come quickly,
please? ...*

Song (based on Psalm 6):

Lord, how long will you tarry?
Come quickly, come to my distress;
in kindness, rescue me from death,
let me see the day when I can praise you.

(From *Psalms of Patience, Protest and Praise* and *Love from Below,* John
L. Bell and Graham Maule)

Reading: John 8:12 (NRSV)

Again Jesus spoke to them, saying, 'I am the light of the world.
Whoever follows me will never walk in darkness but will have the
light of life.'

Prayer:

Loving God, we sometimes walk, sometimes stumble
through life as if it were a waiting room:
as if we were in transit,
waiting for a new day,
a new job, a new task, a new purpose;
waiting for the world
to offer us meaning and value.

As we walk through this
waiting time of Advent,
may we walk in your light,
knowing that this time of Advent waiting can be
active, impatient, radical waiting.
And in this time of waiting may
we be drenched in the plentiful
light of your love.

Amen

Songs of deliverance, 6th December: Worn out with weeping

Song (based on Psalm 6):

I am worn out with grief:
every night confusion fills my mind,
my pillow is soaked with tears
and my eyes are dim and sore with weeping.

(From *Psalms of Patience, Protest and Praise* and *Love from Below,* John
L. Bell and Graham Maule)

Reading: John 11:35

Prayer:

As we weep tears of loneliness and sorrow,
remembering loss and pain and confusion,
may we remember that you, too, wept, dear Lord,
and that our tears of weeping may, and will, one day,
through your transforming love,
turn to tears of joy.

In you we trust.
Amen

Songs of deliverance, 7th December: I trust in the Lord for deliverance

Song (based on Psalm 6):

Lord, you hear how I cry;
the sound of weeping fills your ears.
I trust in you for deliverance
and an end to all that now defeats me.

(From *Psalms of Patience, Protest and Praise* and *Love from Below*, John
L. Bell and Graham Maule)

Reading: John 3:16

Prayer:

God of the morning, we trust you:
in the early dawn of each day,
in the ripening of each new idea,
in the bursting forth of each particle of new light and love,
may we grow in this trust.

God of the noontime, we believe in you:
when we are dazzled by the bright lights
of worldly power and wealth and 'things'
may we remember that you, the God in whom we believe,
comes to us as a refugee with nothing.

God of the evening, our hope is in you:
when all around feels hopeless,
when hope is gone and goodness seems distant,
it is then we remember that
in our darkest night you,
our friend and companion,
halo us with your love.

For this, we praise and thank you.
Amen

Stilling and quiet

Stilling and quiet: A reflection (John)

'It is stillness, I am sure, not the absence of noise, which is the sign of true Friends worship. Stillness is a personal quality, not something in the environment ... The inward stillness which can find God in such a situation is not that of the soul seeking a quiet hour for meditation or reflection. Nor can it come from a mind whose ultimate values are in the world. It is in the stillness that the challenge of the Holy Spirit comes.'

John Punshon [6]

The wisdom, and the practice, of the Society of Friends has always been attractive to me. It's never been a community in which I could see myself belonging, chiefly because I really appreciate the opportunity to sing in worship, and also because I love well-crafted prayers and sermons. And there's also the sense I have that its worship is too heavily intellectual for the individuals and families, and communities too, with whom I've been most involved during my ministry.

That said, what I have grown to appreciate in my admittedly marginal connection with Quaker worship and Quaker practice – as well as their heroic witness to peace and justice over the centuries – is their awareness of *'that of God'* within everyone, and all that flows from that. As I've reflected on that over the years, I've found it echoes time and again in many other spiritual traditions.

Evelyn Underhill, the English mystical writer of the late nineteenth and early twentieth centuries, for example, always stressed *'waiting on God'* as the essential aspect of all Christian action. In her book *The Spiritual Life*, she says:

*'I come now to the many people who, greatly desiring the life of
communion with God, find no opportunity for attention to Him in
existence which lacks privacy, and is conditioned by ceaseless
household duties, exacting professional responsibilities or long
hours of work. The great spiritual writers, who are not nearly so
aloof from normal life as those who do not read them suppose,
have often dealt with this situation ... that what is asked of us is
not necessarily a great deal of time devoted to what we regard as
spiritual things, but the constant offering of our wills to God, so
that the practical duties which fill most of our days can become
part of His order and be given spiritual worth.'*[7]

Behind this I sense the same awareness as that of the Quakers:
that God is to be discerned primarily in waiting, and in stillness,
and that this is not a gift given to a select few, but is available to
everyone.

Sheila Cassidy, writing in *The Tablet* in March 1992, quotes the
poet Ann Lewin on prayer:

*Prayer is like watching for the
Kingfisher. All you can do is
Be where he is likely to appear, and
Wait.
Often, nothing much happens;
There is space, silence and
Expectancy.
No visible sign, only the
Knowledge that he's been there,
And may come again.
Seeing or not seeing cease to matter,
You have been prepared.
But sometimes, when you've almost
Stopped expecting it,*

A flash of brightness
Gives encouragement. [8]

It strikes me that another good analogy is that of the wildlife photographer: sitting sometimes not just for hours but for weeks on end in his or her hide, just to get one fleeting shot of a wild animal, a lynx, or some such very shy creature.

Stillness (Ruth)

'Quiet time', the 30 minutes on a Sunday evening in Iona Abbey, struck me as a child as a complete waste of time. Where was the sense in sitting still, in sitting quiet – when so much joy, delight and wisdom was to be had in running round Tor Abb, in racing through the cloisters, in chat with the staff in the kitchen, or the grounds, or the staffroom? Why be still when all the fibres in my body and soul rushed me to action?!

I do remember Dad once saying that if he hadn't met Mum, he might have become a monk. As a child I thought that was strange – and bizarre, as if that had happened I would not be here! Now I've come to understand. That 'retreat in daily life', that the Ignatian disciplines, that 'the cat and the monkey' carved into the frame of the south window of Iona Abbey – they all reflect the desire of our souls to live between contemplation and action.

After going to my first Quaker Meeting in 1978 with a friend from school, my interest was piqued. For me, a strongly extroverted young person, the discipline of sitting, of waiting within community, was strangely but gloriously familiar. I felt both alien, and that I belonged to a new community.

Weekly Meeting for Worship has brought a new depth to my own spiritual life – and a deep gratitude for the wisdom of the Society of Friends, who together lead me through stillness to radical action for change in our world.

Stillness prayer (John)

Living God,
you always come looking for us,
and your approach
is always one of truth, and of love.
Once again, as Christmas draws near,
you call to us so quietly
from the stories in scripture,
and search for us so lovingly
amidst the busyness and bustle of this time.

Help us to make ready
a straight path for you to travel –
a straight path into our lives,
a straight path into our homes,
a straight path into this small part of the world
over which we have some control.

Living God,
we cannot deny
that we often put obstacles
in the way of your coming.

Too often,
we seem to care more
for scoring points than for telling truth;
too often,
we seem to focus our attention
more on lusting than on loving;
too often,
we seem to care more
for our own wandering ways

than for the straight and narrow path
you seek to set before us.

So forgive us
for our blindness and our obstinacy:
open our whole beings,
body, mind and spirit,
to know your truth
and your love,
and make us ready for you,
once again.

People of God,
the promise to us
is that God forgives us
when we turn back to him.

So we claim that promise now,
in the name of the one who comes,
Jesus of Nazareth, the Christ.
Amen

December 11, 1994, Ruchazie, Glasgow

Whisper meditation and prayers (Ruth)

This meditation and the accompanying prayers were written for the Church of Scotland publication *Word of Life* in 2017. They speak to me now of a time of stillness, of inner quiet amidst a world in turmoil.

What I say to you in the dark, tell in the light;
and what you hear whispered,
proclaim from the housetops.
Matthew 10:26 (NRSV)

And I have learned
to listen

for the whisper of shells
    under the roar of waves;
for the shuffle of a vole
    beneath the leaves;
for the flutter of a breath
    nested in the clamour of the crowd;
for the stillness in my heart
    overcome by need.

And in the listening,
I now know
the power of that
stillness, flutter,
whisper
at the heart of heat:

this is the power of our God
greater than all that can be;
smaller than all that is.

And
this I have come to know:
to trust the whisper –

to raise my voice,
and to raise it quietly.

So let us raise up our voices:
for all wronged;
with the silenced;
where there is fear;
in the face of injustice.

And in this raising up,
let us stay soft,
whisper even,
and so be heard.

Morning prayer:

On this morning, dear Lord,
I pray for the courage to
speak up and speak out
for all who are silenced.

I pray for the insight to know
when a whisper from you
is a nudge to make a difference.

And I pray for the wisdom to discern
those flutters,
whispers of the heart
that are your voice calling me,
now and always.
Amen

Evening prayer:

Loving Lord,
thank you for the day –
for all the good that has been done
quietly,
and for all
the wisdom that has been shared
boldly.

May we know
the gentle flutter
or the raucous roar
that is your
Holy Spirit nudging us
to be bold, speak truth, have no fear.
Amen

Scripture readings:

'... be bold, speak truth, have no fear'

Acts 18:9 (adapted)

'... and after the fire a sound of sheer silence'

1 Kings 19:12 (NRSV)

Blessing:

May the blessing of the God
who whispers 'I love you' and
who shouts 'Be bold'
dwell in our hearts and our hands
now and always.
Amen

Light and dark

Christmas Eve (John)

Reflecting on the crowds pouring into church for a watch night service – Midnight Mass, as it's usually called, by Catholics and Protestants alike, in the West of Scotland – Ron Ferguson wrote:

> *'Semi-detached half-believers, perhaps emboldened by drink, will, in the safety of the crowd on Christmas Eve, sing half-remembered songs full of sentiment and dodgy theology. And some will unexpectedly experience a midnight striking of the hour of grace, a word become flesh in the silent yearning of the heart.'*[9]

For so many of us, isn't this true – that we stumble along on the path of the life of faith, and hopefully, by God's grace, from time to time we will stumble upon that *'word become flesh in the silent yearning of the heart'*?

Across the centuries, a similar wisdom has been captured by others:

First, from St Irenaeus, in the second century AD:

> *'The glory of God is a human being fully alive.'*

Then, from Dietrich Bonhoeffer, eighteen centuries later:

> *'The Christian is not a religious person, but simply a human being, as Jesus was a human being, profoundly this-worldly, characterised by discipline, and the constant knowledge of death and resurrection.'*[10]

And thirdly, from Richard Rohr, the present-day American Franciscan writer and activist:

> *'Jesus did not ask us to worship him; he called us to follow him.'*[11]

Prayer of approach for Christmas Eve (John)

Lord Jesus,
we thank you
that when the world was very dark,
you came,
to bring light into the world.

You came in the night,
bringing light into the lives
of Joseph and Mary.

You came to Bethlehem,
then, as now, a troubled town,
bringing light into the lives
of shepherds and wise men.

And you come to us now,
bringing light still
to all who turn to you.

We ask now
that you will accept the worship
that we bring in return.

As we come again
to the manger
help us to see there
once again
the light that shines for us
and for all people
not just at Christmas
but every day of the year.

We ask this in your name,
and for your sake. Amen

December 24, 2001, Craigsbank, Edinburgh

Birth meditation and prayers (Ruth)

Having experienced the pain, awe and fear of childbirth I am drawn to the story of Mary as she encounters well-meaning supporters imploring her not to be afraid. *'The angel said to her, "Do not be afraid, Mary, for you have found favour with God. And now, you will conceive in your womb and bear a son, and you will name him Jesus"'* (Luke 1:30–31, NRSV). In my first experience of contractions, my epiphanic moment was that pain, and fear, is essential. This feeling, this emotion seems to be designed to say: *'Take care, take very good care. A momentous occasion is taking place. I cannot promise lack of pain. You may even feel fear. But "I am with you" through it all.'*

This meditation and the accompanying prayers were originally written for the Church of Scotland publication *Word of Life* in 2017.[12]

Birth didn't scare me.
It was the talk of others' fears
that shook me.

I didn't think I was afraid.
Then I heard their stories –
grown men who work dark nights,
comforted by angels: 'Do not be afraid.'

I didn't think I was afraid.
Then he shared his dream –
my beloved,
reassured by visions: 'Do not be afraid.'

I didn't think I was afraid.
Then they said:
'Do not return home.'

And now, I am afraid …

… I fear for this child and our lives,
on the run, uncertain, fleeing
from the fear-power-driven
recklessness of those
unprepared to trust;
unsure of
their place in the world.

In these uncertain times
I choose to remember
that the fear of those
lost in reckless power
is overturned
by the magnitude of the love
our God has for us.

And so I return to my fearlessness,
and trust in the angels who said:
'Do not be afraid.'

Morning prayer:

May we this day
live with the fearlessness of Mary
and the courage of the shepherds,
who, in the face of their fears,
nevertheless trusted the angels
and followed
their hearts' yearnings.

As we face our fears today and daily,
may we know the magnitude
of God's love.
May this love
spill out from our hearts
and transform all who
live in real fear for their lives
and their loved ones.

This we pray in the name of Jesus.
Amen

Evening prayer:

Oh my soul,
as I turn to the night
to the dreams and the dark,
may I re-fill with hope and love,
and so turn again to the morning
renewed and inspired
to live in the love of You,
Risen Jesus.
Amen

Scripture readings:

Genesis 26:24: God reassures Isaac

Acts 18:9: Paul is given courage from the Lord, 'Do not be afraid, but speak, be bold.'

Blessing:

The blessing of the God of love
be on us and on all we love,
today, and always. Amen

Lent

Introduction (John and Ruth)

If Christmas is about mystery, Lent is more about a challenge to our humanity. We are both regularly challenged by those from within the Muslim community who are our friends, neighbours and colleagues, who respond so profoundly to the physical commitments inherent in Ramadan. A conversation John had with a Muslim friend comes to mind. When he asked about what John did during Lent, the reply about giving up chocolate seemed incredibly lame, while during Ramadan John's friend worked a full day without anything to eat or drink, eating only when he returned home after sunset. This approach to fasting, and the physical, as well as spiritual, demands it makes on our humanity sits in stark contrast to the often more symbolic actions that many Christians practise in Lent. The witness of our Muslim brothers and sisters seems to honour a much more robust approach to discipline.

As a representative of the Protestant Churches at the annual World Orthodox Youth Assembly in Greece in the early 1990s, Ruth had an experience of the human challenge of fasting:

We had spent the best part of a week together, over 150 Orthodox youth from around the world. And me! I had made friends, engaged in deep conversation about faith, politics, church, liturgy and the ecumenical movement. We had shared daily worship and grown in our sense of belonging together. On the last day we were to fast and pray, only breaking the fast at midnight during Holy Communion. I had never experienced fasting as intensely before, and to share this as a collective experience was powerful. In denying my body food I came keenly to understand what I needed for nourishment. The parallel with my spiritual life was immense: in times of spiritual denial, when I restrict time for prayer, reflection, connection with the Divine mystery, I become acutely aware of the loss, the hunger deep inside.

As midnight grew closer, and hunger and tiredness gripped my body and soul, I yearned for food – any food! And most crucially, for the blessed bread and wine of Holy Communion. Never had I been more ready to receive. Standing, therefore, for three hours, taking part in the liturgy in multiple foreign languages, none of which I understood, only heightened my desire for food, for nourishment. When, at 3am, as I ought to have predicted as a theologian, and as a Protestant in an Orthodox setting, the bread and wine passed me by, I felt the depth of hunger and of separation as an acute, profound pain. The compassion and shared tears of my friends in that community may have served to lessen the blow of physical discomfort but only heighted the scandal of ecumenical separation.

Bearing the pain of exclusion, the pain of broken communion, and of broken human community, is part of the essence of being human. Living in community with others who are different from us – who bring different experiences and traditions, and who at the same time can honour and respect one another while experiencing each other's uniqueness or 'otherness' – is a gift. At times such as Lent, when we strip away some of life's excesses, we experience more fully the depth of connection, and the scandal of separation built by human institutions.

Reflecting on brokenness and wholeness during Lent brings us into contact not only with the brokenness within our theologies, but with the brokenness in our churches and our communities. Since 2009, both as a volunteer and as a staff member, Ruth has been involved with the work of Place for Hope, supporting congregations and faith communities seeking reconciliation. The pain, and often the guilt, of disagreement in a community 'where we all love one another' are dynamics familiar to Place for Hope's skilled team of volunteer Practitioners. A profound learning gained through this work is the knowledge of the extent of the weight of despair and anxiety that many in our faith communities feel, the guilt that they don't live up to what is expected of them. When we open up the Gospel stories of the early church, of Jesus' ministry, or Paul's letters, we read together of a vibrant, growing church full of brokenness and wholeness: broken and whole human beings and human communities.

In the Iona Community, we love one another. But this does not necessarily mean that we must also always *like* one another! We see our holy imperfections writ large on a daily basis as we negotiate rotas, passions and tiredness. George MacLeod, on the call to discipline, said: '*If you can walk without a crutch, good for you – I can't!*' We may not be perfect, but in our imperfection we are good enough. Maybe this is what it means to be fully, perfectly human.

On temptation and living by faith

The temptations of Jesus (John)

As I reflect on some of the aspects of the life of Jesus, I wonder how Jesus dealt with temptation – the temptations in the wilderness, and the final huge temptation in the Garden of Gethsemane. The way these stories are presented in the Gospel, you could easily think that these temptations really were no big deal – Jesus knew they were coming, he knew how to handle them, he handled them, bingo!

Reading *Addiction and Grace,* by Gerald May, the late American psychiatrist and theologian, got me thinking about how I handle – or rather struggle to handle (and so often failing) – temptations when they come. This in turn has led to the realisation of just what a huge struggle it must have been for Jesus.

In the wilderness, for Heaven's sake, Jesus must have surely toyed with the three possibilities that 'Satan' put before him – imagined himself as really being able to feed all the hungry, imagined himself as really being able to wow all the people by throwing himself off the temple roof and being held up by angels, imagined himself as really becoming King of the World, just by agreeing to worship Satan.

And these would have been real, existential possibilities in his mind – not just paper temptations – real hard and attractive possibilities – against which he had to struggle with everything he had. No wonder it says in the Gospel that when he faced the final temptation in the Garden he prayed so hard that the sweat broke out on his forehead *'like drops of blood'* – for he must actually have been imagining what it would be like NOT to allow himself to be crucified – to go on and live out a decent and respectable life, perhaps get married, have a family, be loved and adored by many, and die in his bed.

To say 'No' to that, and instead go willingly to a horrible death – as I say, no wonder he sweated blood! We preachers focus so much on the outcome of his struggle, perhaps, that we don't concentrate enough on the actual struggle itself. And surely we should – because it's a struggle that millions face every day – sometimes winning, more often losing, but sweating over it, day in, day out. We all need all the help we can get in this struggle – and God surely offers us such help in the life of Jesus.

This time and this place: Opening prayer (John)

Living God,
help us now.
Here is a time for us
to focus away from ourselves
and onto you.
Here is a place for us
to look away from our places
and look to yours.
Here is a community of your people,
called together
not by our common interest
but by your gracious word.

So,
in the quietness of this time
and of this place
and of this community,
help us to be open
to your Spirit.

Living God,
you are always
the God of surprises.
When we have thought to find you
only in a special time,
a special place,
you have asked us to look for you
in every time, every place.

When we have thought to confine you
to one special group of people,
or one particular creed or custom,
you have taught us
that you are to be found
amongst all people, everywhere.

So here,
in this special time and place,
and amongst this special people,
help us to celebrate once again
that because you are here, you are everywhere:
all life is yours,
all the world your dwelling place,
every human heart
potentially your home.

Lord Jesus,
desert-dweller,
in this time of Lent,
we would accompany you.
If we have grown soft,
cushioning our lives with excuses,

expose us again
to the toughness of your way.

If we have grown lazy,
cushioning our minds with easy shallow thoughts,
expose us again
to the rigour of your truth.

If we have grown comfortable,
cushioning our living
with satisfaction and success,
expose us again
to the challenge of your life.

And as we walk,
God, be our way;

as we learn,
God, be our truth;

as we grow,
God, be our life.

We pray in Jesus' name. Amen

March 12th, 2000

Living by faith in the world (John)

The most influential of all my teachers was Ronald Gregor Smith,
Professor of Divinity at Glasgow University. He opened my mind
to a whole new way of understanding the Gospel. Bonhoeffer, Bult-
mann and Buber were huge influences on him, and so on us all.

His book *The New Man*, published in 1956, the year he took

up the Chair at Glasgow, is a truly prophetic piece of writing. Here is one passage from it:

> 'God is met in his gifts and works, not in himself, and not in an idea of him. He is met at the luminous point of human existence, where the individual faces him in utter openness, receives forgiveness, and is made free.' [13]

It was the 19th-century Quaker, William Littleboy, who wrote *'to be a Christian consists not in feeling but in following; not in ecstasy but in obedience'*; a neat little epigram, perhaps a touch too neat, but nevertheless pointing up, for me, the founding aspect of the life of faith, which the Iona Community has encapsulated in its advice to us all to *'follow the light you see, and pray for more light'*.

I've often used the analogy, which I got, again, from the Iona Community, of a person being shut up, alone, in a large darkened room, with only a handheld candle for light, and needing to get across to the other side of the room in safety. If the person stands still and tries to see the obstacles in their path simply by holding up the candle and peering into the darkness, then they will never get across; it's only by beginning to walk forward that the candle will reveal the obstacles to be avoided, and thus get them to the other side.

Abbé G. Michonneau was a French Roman Catholic priest in Paris in the 1940s, and a founder of the Worker Priest Movement, encouraging young priests to go to Germany to work as labourers alongside the thousands of young Frenchmen who were forced to go there to work by the occupying Nazis. He said something like *when God gives us light for the road ahead, it's not the light of street lamps that we're talking about, but the light from the headlamps of a car – and that only illuminates the road ahead as you keep moving!*

So we are to move forward in the life of faith with courage, remembering Julian of Norwich's advice: *'He said not "Thou shalt not be tempested, thou shalt not be travailed, thou shalt not be diseased"; but he said "Thou shalt not be overcome"'.* [14]

For someone like me, brought up in a tightly controlled environment, and with a built-in predilection for having everything under control, this moving forward with courage is not something I've always been very good at. Again through the Iona Community, I've seen how issues have been moved forward very effectively often by individuals who are passionate about them – like Helen Steven on peace and justice, John Bell on liturgy, and of course George MacLeod himself on a number of issues – just getting on and doing things, and not waiting until everyone else is on board alongside them. I guess my inclination has rather been to try to get others on board first before making a move – which had the advantage of broad ownership of the concern involved, but the disadvantage of caution and dilution.

Then along comes St Augustine again, with this great phrase:

'Hope has two beautiful daughters. Their names are Anger and Courage: anger at the way things are, and courage to see that they do not remain the way they are.'

Jim Wallis of Sojourners echoes this sentiment with his *'hope is believing in spite of the evidence, and then watching the evidence change'.* [15] And Wallis offers a further wise word for the serious-minded activists among us who sometimes feel that it's always up to us to change the world: *'The marks of grace are gentleness, hope and faith. The most dependable sign of its presence is joy.'* [16]

Faithfulness in the desert: Opening prayer (John)

Living, faithful God,
help us to worship you now.

We remember your faithfulness
to your people Israel,
even in the midst
of their unfaithfulness to you.
You led them out of captivity
to live in responsible freedom;
and though they turned from you,
or sought to remake you in their image,
you never deserted them.

We remember your faithfulness
in Jesus,
even in the midst
of the unfaithfulness all around him.
Through him,
you have shown us all the way
out of the captivity of our past
and into the responsible freedom
of the new life he brings.

So we would worship you now
and offer you the praise
of our lips and of our lives.

Living God, at this time
we remember again
that going up to Jerusalem
cost Jesus his very life.
So we come before you
very conscious of the way

religious words and pious phrases
can slip so easily
from our lazy lips
and our selfish hearts.

What do we really know
of your mountainous truth,
your rock-hard integrity,
the depth of your suffering
for the love of each one of us?

Forgive us
for the shallowness of our faith,
and the timidity of our following;
forgive us
for the ready excuses we make
for going our own way
and claiming it to be yours.

Send us once again
that same Spirit
who was in Jesus:
the Spirit of fortitude,
the Spirit of faithfulness,
the Spirit of forgiveness,
the Spirit of New Life,
that we may follow once again,
in courage, faith and cheerfulness,
on the Way of the Cross.

We ask this in his name.

Amen

1st April, 2001

On transformation and theologies of reconciliation

Praying through conflict (Ruth)[17]

'Conflict opens a path, a holy path, towards revelation and reconciliation.'

John Paul Lederach [18]

In the work that Place for Hope do with churches and faith communities we believe in the positive transformative power of conflict. We affirm, with John Paul Lederach, that conflict can open up *'a path, a holy path'*, towards inner and outer transformation. We also acknowledge that working with conflict can be tough. When conflict is transformed and relationships are healed, we offer prayers of thanks, gratitude and joy. In the midst of conflict, however, where we experience deep darkness, intransigence, separation and violence even, we turn to a different kind of prayer: prayers of anguish and despair; prayers for help.

In prayer, we turn towards God, ask for help and remain open to a response. When we find ourselves in a broken relationship, in a divided community, in a church at loggerheads, or overwhelmed by the violence and war in the world, the same three-fold prayer dynamic persists: *turn to God, ask for help, and remain open to the surprise of the Holy Spirit.*

In prayer, turn to God

In turning to God in times of conflict we immediately acknowledge that we are not alone. No matter how wise we are as human beings, in prayer we acknowledge a deeper, wider mystery of faith that brings peace to strife. The very act of turning to God can itself be the start of a process of reconciliation: in turning, we turn inwards to the wisdom of God found in stillness, prayer, times of quiet meditation. In turning, we turn outwards, opening ourselves to the possibility that new ways may be found to respond to conflict, difference and change in the future – both in ourselves and in the other. Turning outwards, we may find ourselves turning to face the one who is our enemy – and in this way, find ourselves on the path to transformation.

In turning to God we find ourselves praying: 'In you, O Lord, I put my trust.' And in this way, we may discover anew the wisdom of the Lord's Prayer: *'your kingdom come, your will be done'*. In turning to God in conflict, we begin by asking: 'What is your will, dear God?'

In prayer, ask for help

The Psalms tell many stories of enemies, hatred, revenge killing and the abuse of power. These are stories with echoes in our own era. Yet scripture, and the Psalms, also reveal to us the persistence and faith of God's people who, in times of awful trouble, continue to turn to God in prayer for help. Psalm 46 sets the tone with *'God is our refuge and our strength, a very present help in trouble.'* This ever-present God is affirmed again in Matthew 18 when, in a chapter full of conflict, we read *'where two or three are gathered in my name, I am there among them'*, or in other words, 'when you are in trouble, and you ask for my help, know that I am already there among you'. This may not mean that events will turn out as we wish, or expect – but we can be sure that when we ask for help in prayer, we will receive it, and we are not alone.

In prayer, remain open to the surprise of the Holy Spirit

In Genesis 25, Isaac and Rebekah are surprised when their prayers for a child are answered by the miracle of twins. However, they may have been equally surprised by the ensuing terrible conflict between their boys – and then, finally, their reconciliation.

The story of the reconciliation of Jacob and Esau, who could have been destined to become sworn enemies, gives us hope: the experience of humiliation by 'the other', of running away from our enemy, and then, with God's help, of finding the strength to turn to greet the enemy are all present in this story.

As we remain open in prayer to the surprise of the Holy Spirit, we may discover that what seems to be an intractable and unbearable conflict carries within it deeper truths that can transform our lives and the lives of those around us.

In times of conflict it can be helpful to:

- take time to be still;

- turn to God in openness and humility;

- seek the help of God, and of others around you, to understand the differences that face you;

- be prepared to be surprised by the gift of the Holy Spirit;

- trust that conflict can *'open up a holy path'* to transformation.

Prayers (sourced by John)

A prayer of intercession for Gorbals (from the Gorbals Group, sourced by John)

Let us bring to God
the needs of His world,
remembering especially the people of this place,
in their homes, in the streets, and at their work.

(A time of silent remembering)

Lord Christ, we uphold your people for mercy and for blessing.

By your healing of the diseased,
Lord, heal the sick.

By your fortitude in the storm,
Lord, calm the fearful.

By your fondness for little children,
Lord, protect the young.

By your labour at a bench,
Lord, hallow our work.

By your forgiveness on the cross,
Lord, pardon our sins.

By your rising from the dead,
Lord, give us life.

A Hebrew blessing (from Psalm 115)

May you be blessed by the Lord,
the Maker of heaven and earth.
The heavens belong to the Lord
but to us he has given the earth.
The dead shall not praise the Lord,
nor those who go down into the silence.
But we who live bless the Lord,
now and for ever. Amen

Meditations and prayers for unity in the midst of pain (Ruth)[19]

As part of a writers' group from Churches Together in Britain and Ireland (CTBI), I have been privileged to work on material for the annual worldwide 'Week of Prayer for Christian Unity'. Each year source material is provided by a council of churches from a region or nation of the world. Our CTBI group then meets in retreat-like space to deepen and broaden our understanding of the texts and the context, and so our commitment to unity.

The first five meditations here were inspired by source material prepared by churches in Germany focusing on the 500th anniversary of the German Reformation, in 2017. The sixth meditation was inspired by source material prepared by Churches Together in the Caribbean for 2018, and in Jamaica in particular, as they reflected on how the 'hand of God' supports and upholds their common life – including being a healing presence in a world of violence. The seventh and final meditation and prayer were inspired by source material prepared by our friends in the churches of Indonesia.

I. Friendship

(Isaiah 53:4–12; Psalm 118:1, 14–29; 1 John 2:1–2; John 15:13–17)

If this is friendship …
… to discover light through anguish;
… to overcome punishment with wholeness;
… to embrace healing through
being bruised and crushed
tortured and killed;

if he died in this way,
for us

his friends,
for once, for all;
then can I believe?

II. Re-source

(Micah 6:6–8; Psalm 15:1–5; 1 John 4:19–21; Matthew 16:24–26)

Like entering a new galaxy,
in order to find my source
must I first lose all sense of self?

Is not the paradox of self-loss that
in order fully to find the other
first I must know, love and embrace self?

Only then may I fold my self
into the great galaxy of the 'I am'.

III. Re-human

(1 Samuel 16:1, 6–7; Psalm 19:7–13; Acts 9:1–19; Matthew 5:1–12)

Is it possible that
we have de-humanised
terrified children and
fleeing mothers
for the sake of tranquillity?

Is it possible that
we have be-littled
ourselves so much
that reality means more
through a screen
than a touch?

Is it possible that
we have been seen
so completely
that through a slight-seismic
Saul/Paul shift
our divinity becomes more visible
than our humanity?

IV. Re-member

(Genesis 19:15–26; Psalm 77:5–15; Philippians 3:7–14; Luke 9:57–62)

To linger over-long
in the haze of time,
so stifling the past
in nostalgia
or blame-fuelled fury,
en-shrouds, tomb-like,
as with salt,
moments otherwise free to soar.

But to re-imagine the past,
leaning deep into memory,
so freeing the now
to birth the not yet

to draw out
flavours of the future,
as with salt,
to taste and see goodness ...

now this is how it is
to re-member.

V. *Covenant*

(Ezekiel 36:25–27; Psalm 126; Colossians 3:9–17; John 3:1–8)

This I do not know:
whether I must change, repent – reform
before reaching for reconciliation;
or if, rather,
being reconciled with my
brothers and sisters
is a necessary condition
for reformation.

This I know:
that human time,
rarely straight-lining,
rather, spirals;
that the troublesome
grit-of-separation
seeps into the cavities
of the walls of division,
growing layers of wisdom:
pearls of reconciliation.

And this more I know:
that the covenant
binding us with God
is a gift of God's time.

VI. *Hope and healing*

(Isaiah 9:2–7a; Psalm 34:1–14; Revelation 7:13–17; John 14:25–27)

In our beautiful (is)land
violence breeds violence
('an eye for an eye …')
and abuse, murder, rape
('limb from limb …')
become a way of life
as teenage bodies are ravaged beyond repair,
neighbourhoods are gang-violated,
and lives abused –
domestically.
('heads dashed against rock'?)

We see.
We know,
and we wail: 'For the love of God. In the name of Jesus. Stop.'

The hand of God stretches into pain saying:
'I bring comfort, justice, righteousness,'
and we remember that
veiled by the violence,
obscured by our walled communities,
beneath the facade of this island-idyll
lie true all-inclusive packages of
beauty

seen and known
by our God of hope.
Each single sacramental life,
precious beyond measure,
is made whole
in the healing
hand of God.

We believe that
in the paradise-heaven
as close to us as the waves lapping our golden shores
there is
no hunger
no thirst
no torching of lives
or scorching of earth.

Here our tears are wiped away.
Springs of living water
revive our worn-out bodies,
our weary earth.

VII. *'Let your words be "Yes, yes", or "No, no"'*

(Matthew 5:37)

If I am to speak truth to power,
whose truth do I speak?
Whose justice do I seek
in the liminal space between my right-ness
    and that of the 'other'.

If I say 'yes' to justice,
does that make it all mine?
What of the grey between the emphatics?
'Let me
declare boldly,
sure-footedly
that my yes is
a "yes-yes", and my
no is "no",' says Jesus.

'Let me
draw clarity
in the sand that
defines and refines
knowledge, truth and tales
in such a way
that all are sure.

'Let me
dwell deep
in the place within
where, regardless of the outward form,
you know beyond doubt's shadow,
that truth and justice,
peace and righteousness lie.

'And let me,
in my boldness,
turn widdershins
the hypocrisy of
those who confuse integrity with fake-ness,
who obscure truth with falsehood
and call it news.

'Let me boldly be
good news.'

Prayer

God of justice,
grant me the wisdom to see right from wrong.
Let my heart be guided by honesty and my lips speak truth.
In times of doubt, cloak me in courage the colour of trust.

Birth in me the agency of unity and peace
so that I may be a good news bearer for all.
In Jesus' name I pray.
Amen

The Reformation and conflict: Reflections for Lent 2017 (Ruth)

Gospel reading: John 3:1–17 (NRSV)

Now there was a Pharisee named Nicodemus, a leader of the Jews. He came to Jesus by night and said to him, 'Rabbi, we know that you are a teacher who has come from God; for no one can do these signs that you do apart from the presence of God.'

Jesus answered him, 'Very truly, I tell you, no one can see the kingdom of God without being born from above.' Nicodemus said to him, 'How can anyone be born after having grown old? Can one enter a second time into the mother's womb and be born?' Jesus answered, 'Very truly, I tell you, no one can enter the kingdom of God without being born of water and Spirit. What is born of the flesh is flesh, and what is born of the Spirit is spirit. Do not be astonished that I said to you, "You must be born from above." The wind blows where it chooses, and you hear the sound of it, but you do not know where it comes from or where it goes. So it is with everyone who is born of the Spirit.' Nicodemus said to him, 'How can these things be?' Jesus answered him, 'Are you a teacher of Israel, and yet you do not understand these things?

'Very truly, I tell you, we speak of what we know and testify to what we have seen; yet you do not receive our testimony. If I have told you about earthly things and you do not believe, how can you believe if I tell you about heavenly things? No one has ascended into heaven except the one who descended from heaven, the Son of Man. And just as Moses lifted up the serpent in the wilderness, so must the Son of Man be lifted up, that whoever believes in him may have eternal life.

'For God so loved the world that he gave his only Son, so that everyone who believes in him may not perish but may have eternal life.

'Indeed, God did not send the Son into the world to condemn the world, but in order that the world might be saved through him.'

Reading from the Epistles: Romans 11:32–36 (NRSV)

For God has imprisoned all in disobedience so that he may be merciful to all.

O the depth of the riches and wisdom and knowledge of God! How unsearchable are his judgements and how inscrutable his ways!

'For who has known the mind of the Lord?
Or who has been his counsellor?'
'Or who has given a gift to him,
to receive a gift in return?'

For from him and through him and to him are all things. To him be the glory forever. Amen

Sermon/reflection

On this second Sunday in the season of Lent, and in this 500th year of a reforming Church, I offer three short invitations into a 'Spirituality of conflict'.

I'll draw on the story of the night-time meeting between Jesus and Nicodemus in the Gospel of John. I'll also draw on the work of Place for Hope, a charity which supports churches and faith communities through times of change and conflict.

And if you're wondering what on earth a 'spirituality of conflict' might be – take yourself to the website of that name – it's a collaboration between Place for Hope, the Corrymeela Community, the Iona Community, the Church of Scotland and a number of others. Through this project we are exploring the stories of the Bible, and in particular the teachings of Jesus and how we can understand, and respond to, conflict through the lens of the Gospel. Readings, prayers and reflections are offered from this ecumenical group as we draw wisdom from the Gospel into our world where our divisions and differences continue to breed conflict, violence and war.

If our spirituality is *'that which ultimately moves us'* (Kathy Galloway), then we would say that given that conflict is a normal part of our common human condition, let us together seek from our spiritual paths the wisdom that can respond to, and transform, conflict for the good of the world.

Our Gospel reading is essentially the story of two men who ought to be in deep conflict. One, Nicodemus, the leader in the Sanhedrin community and a Pharisee; the other, Jesus, the leader of a rebel, seemingly uncontrollable sect.

Nicodemus would have been settling in for a deep theological conversation with Jesus about what it meant to be saved – assuming, as was the norm among his Jewish community, that those who needed to be saved were Gentiles. Jesus' message was at best confusing – at worst deeply unsettling for Nicodemus. *'Truly, I tell you, no one can enter the kingdom of God without being born of water and Spirit.'*

Conversion, being born again – re-forming – was essential for everyone, Nicodemus included.

The darkness of the night, surrounding the men, and surrounding their conversation, perhaps reflects the uncertainty of the times – both religious and political. Times not unlike our own times of religious and political flux. And perhaps not so unlike the time of the reformers we are thinking of this Lent, such as Martin Luther, John Calvin and John Knox.

In Place for Hope, we talk about conflict *transformation*, rather than conflict resolution, or even conflict mediation.

We focus on the transformational potential of conflict because:

• we think conflict is normal and is there to be embraced;

• we recognise that in embracing conflict, life may never be the same again – we may be transformed;

• we recognise the remarkable gift in our churches, and our faith communities, filled with great spiritual leaders who understand the power of re-formation and transformation.

So, to the three invitations on this Lenten journey:

The first invitation to a spirituality of conflict that is offered to us through this text is to a reformation of the heart – *an inner transformation*. Both Jesus and Nicodemus were willing, despite the conflict between themselves and their faith tradition, to enter into a conversation about the depth, and differences, of their faith. The art of honest, gracious conversation with someone different from ourselves is a crucial first step in conflict transformation. As is the art of honest, gracious conversation with ourselves about how we respond to conflict.

In Place for Hope, as we accompany congregations and faith-based organisations through change, transition and conflict, we begin with a focus on inner transformation. Henri Nouwen has written on the call to be a *'wounded healer'*; that to be a healer of others, it's first important that we know what it means to heal ourselves, to be in need of our own healing.

And so it is with conflict transformation.

To be a healer of conflict, first it's crucial to know what conflict feels like from within – to explore our own inner woundedness, and to understand our own responses to conflict.

Archbishop Justin Welby, struggling with an Anglican communion deeply divided over the issue of human sexuality, talked of the need for the church to be full of *'reconciled recon-cilers'*. To be a conflict reconciler, we need first to be reconciled people – at peace with God, and with ourselves.

This invitation also, of course, comes to us directly from Jesus when he invites us to *'love your neighbour as you love yourself'*.

As Presbyterians it can sometimes be all too easy to skip the second of these invitations and to focus almost solely on what it means to 'love your neighbour', ignoring that this is based on the love of self. For some, good works means direct action: feeding the homeless, eradicating poverty. For others, good works means reforming the church: taking up our responsibilities on commit-tees, engaging in political action. And all this 'good work' is crucial to the lived mission of our church: we must *'be the hands of God in the world'*: love our neighbour.

But Jesus said …'love your neighbour *as you love yourself'*.

The invitation from Jesus to each of us today, as it was to Nicodemus, is to inner reformation.

Perhaps this was the gentleness nested within Jesus' response to Nicodemus: 'Your statements, your boldness in the night-time – I can hear all of this. But, Nicodemus, here's the thing – be bold inwardly, come to me with vulnerability, with humility, and your riches will increase exponentially.'

And Jesus then invites Nicodemus into the astonishing journey of being born again – inner reformation.

If we can love ourselves, be gentle with ourselves, be honest with ourselves about our own responses to conflict, then the transformation, the 'born-again-ness' we seek in the world will be so much more sustaining and sustainable.

An example of this is shown during Place for Hope's 'Growing through change and conflict' training day. First we invite partici-pants to consider their own response to conflict: 'do I use a direc-ting, an avoiding, a compromising style more naturally?', and so on. Regularly, we meet church leaders eager to skip this invitation and move straight into the afternoon session, focused on how we can help others in our churches transform conflict. Usually around lunchtime there is a moment of realisation when participants become aware that we can't become 'reconcilers' until we are first at least aware of our own ongoing need for reconciliation.

The second invitation to a spirituality of conflict this gospel text offers is to the reformation of our church – *a journey in community*. For both Nicodemus and Jesus were deeply engaged in shaping their own particular faith communities.

For deep transformation to take place, we need leaders in our churches, lay and ordained, willing to set aside the particularities of our own faith traditions to focus on a deeper, wider, broader unity, or *oikoumene*, which transcends and embraces all difference.

When Place for Hope works with groups, we initially agree ways to ensure that our gathering will be effective. These are agreements to which we will hold one another in the course of our work. They can act as a steady rock while all else may seem fluid. One of these agreements is that we will listen to 'one voice at a time'. This means that when one person is speaking, others listen. Full attention is given to the speaker. This also means 'stilling the voice in our head'. There may be no one else speaking, but the voice in our head may be rehearsing a response, a reaction, a refute to what has been said.

To respond to this invitation to church reformation (from a church whose motto is *'church always in need of reform'*) I have these questions:

As we search for peace and unity in the world church, are we prepared to sit lightly to the structures of our own particular tradition in order to reach for a greater sense of belonging to the universal church?

> *How closely are we willing to work with, or even merge with, our sisters and brothers in other Christian denominations to live close to Jesus' call for unity?*

And finally, the third invitation a spirituality of conflict offers is participation in *a global reformation.*

In the night-time of our world – that liminal space between deep day and deep night – we might experience, like Nicodemus, a sense of vulnerability, anxiety, uncertainty.

Our legacy as Christians in the world can often be marred with violent stories of crusade, abuse and ongoing revelations of bullying and aggression. For these things, and for much more in our troubled history, we must ask, and continue to ask, for forgiveness. And we must mend the past, and change our present behaviour for the sake of us all, so that all may truly feel included.

Alongside these stories of violence which we must not ignore – and let's not pretend that the Reformation was a peaceful affair – there are also many stories of peacemakers of faith. If the church needs spiritual leaders, at ease with conflict, difference and diversity, then our world needs these leaders even more.

And of course each one of us can be a 'reconciling reconciler', or 'global elder', as each one of us is called by God to be a peacemaker.

To be invited into a spirituality of conflict is:

- first, to be invited into *an inner transformation* of the heart, to become a 'reconciling reconciler';

- secondly, to be invited into *a transformation of the church community*, where we have leaders at ease with conflict, difference and diversity;

- and thirdly, to be invited into *a global transformation*, where the hallmark is forgiveness for all the wrongs we have wrought in the past, a forgiveness, both sought and offered, and so a truly global transformation of our world to one of justice, peace, truth and mercy.

And it is in this spirit, and in the name of our transforming, forgiving God known to us in Jesus, that *'we lay our broken world in sorrow at the feet of God'*.[20] Amen

On hope and possibilities

Live in the Light: Reflections on peacemaking and reconciliation (Ruth)

Introduction:

> *'Be patterns, be examples in all countries, places, islands, nations, wherever you come, that your carriage and life may preach among all sorts of people, and to them; then you will come to walk cheerfully over the world, answering that of God in everyone.'*

– George Fox, 1656, from Advices & Queries [21]

Advices & Queries is a summary of the wisdom of the Yearly Meeting of the Religious Society of Friends (Quakers) in Britain. '*A reminder of the insights of the Society*', these As&Qs have been gathered and modified through experience since the late seventeenth century. Within their 42 brief paragraphs, they offer guidance for the individual worshipper, for the community of believers and for each of us all, alone and in community, as we engage in the concerns for peace, justice, equality, simplicity and right relationship in the world.

In the following five reflections I have selected excerpts that 'speak to my condition' in the hope that they may also 'speak' to yours (and have suggested further paragraphs that may also be useful). I have followed the pattern of beginning with inner reconciliation, moving through reconciliation in our worshipping community or church, to reconciliation in the world. For a complete (free) copy of *Advices & Queries* visit www.quaker.org.uk.

1. Inwardly reconciled: 'Cherish that of God within you'

'Bring the whole of your life under the ordering of the spirit of Christ. Are you open to the healing power of God's love? Cherish that of God within you, so that this love may grow in you and guide you. Let your worship and your daily life enrich each other. Treasure your experience of God, however it comes to you. Remember that Christianity is not a notion but a way.'

(Advices & Queries 2. See also 1, 3, 4, 7, 11, 28, 31 and 32)

Being a 'reconciled reconciler' is a lifelong journey – first we are invited to be reconciled with ourselves – with all those parts of our self we struggle to embrace, those character traits that we perhaps even deny, or push away.

The God of love loves each part of us, for God is within and without. To be a healer, it helps to know how it feels to be in need of healing. To be a peacemaker, it helps to know how it feels to be at war with oneself. To be a reconciler, it helps to know how it feels to be reconciled to oneself. To love our neighbour as we love ourselves, first we must know what it means to love our self from the inside out. In so much of Christendom it may seem counter-cultural to focus on the self, to be mindful of the peace that Christ wishes for each one of us. But Jesus spoke of living in the present, of embracing the kingdom, present now within each one of us.

- *John Knox spoke of 'the notes of Presbyterianism': the core, resonating identities that give that tradition its singularity. What is the 'note' that resonates most deeply within you?*

- *When, and in what contexts, do you feel unquestionably cherished by God? Notice these times. Nurture, welcome and encourage them. For it is out of this space of inner peace that we are more able to become peacemakers in the world.*

2. Resilient and calm: 'Live adventurously'

> 'Live adventurously. When choices arise, do you take the way that offers the fullest opportunity for the use of your gifts in the service of God and the community? Let your life speak. When decisions have to be made, are you ready to join with others in seeking clearness, asking for God's guidance and offering counsel to one another?'

(Advices & Queries 27. *See also* 28, 41)

With the children in our local Quaker meeting we explored what it might mean to 'live adventurously'. For some, this meant planning and taking trips to wild parts of the country. For others, living adventurously meant standing up to school bullies, speaking 'truth to power', coming forward with ideas rather than holding back. Yet others reflected that to live adventurously would mean to give up busyness. Comfort in activity can mask a deeper discomfort in stillness. To stop, seek out stillness in busy lives may lead us on an inner adventure.

Margaret Silf, in her book *Inner Compass* (Loyola Press), offers a simple, Ignatius-inspired exercise for discerning how to live adventurously. She invites us first to reflect on 'the givens' in our lives, those things that we cannot change: our genetics, the place and time of our birth ...

After reflecting on these, try to set them to one side, she says. Next, she invites us to reflect on those areas of life over which we have choice: maybe work, location, use of time ... and then to set these aside. Finally, she invites us to reflect on what remains: the core, the inner identity, who we are at root once the outer layers of happenstance and choice have been set aside for a while. She suggests that it is out of this inner 'I am' that we encounter the immanent God, the God who dwells within. And from this inner place of clarity, the 'God-seed' can grow and flourish – and we can then 'live adventurously' in the world.

This, I think, is the 'clearness' of which Quakers speak: an inner clarity that speaks through the everyday.

- *What does 'live adventurously' mean to you?*

- *How do you seek God's guidance in your decisions?*

- *How open are you to any surprise that may emerge as you wait?*

- *What comfort zones do you inhabit?*

- *What could nudge you out of familiar patterns?*

3. Reconciliation in community: 'Think it possible that you may be mistaken'

'Do you respect that of God in everyone though it may be expressed in unfamiliar ways or be difficult to discern? Each of us has a particular experience of God and each must find the way to be true to it. When words are strange or disturbing to you, try to sense where they come from and what has nourished the lives of others. Listen patiently and seek the truth which other people's opinions may contain for you. Avoid hurtful criticism and provocative language. Do not allow the strength of your convictions to betray you into making statements or allegations that are unfair or untrue. Think it possible that you may be mistaken.'

(Advices & Queries 17. *See also* 22 and 26)

Dear Lord,
we pray for a round table –
a United Nations negotiating table;
a Number 10 oval office table;
a communion kitchen table –
any such sacramental table.

A table where the corners have been replaced by curves,
and where the stuff (and word) of life is blessed and sent around
(like salt and spice),
where the Holy Spirit loops the bend to rest –
these are holy round tables:
places of reconciliation.

For reconciliation
to come around,
give us grace, good Lord,
to notice our stolid square-ness;
then so much more grace
to embrace the complete 'round' in ourselves.

Where rough edges
have been smoothed,
where hard opinions
have been softened,
we give you thanks that
here is
the space
for reconciling love.

Amen [22]

4. Peace in the church

'Take time to learn about other people's experience of the Light.'

(*Extract from* Advices & Queries 5. *See also 6, 14, 18 and 22*)

It was a warm summer's day and we were resting from our work. A team from across Europe had joined together for a summer language school, while also building a new sauna for the local community ('*a demanding common task alone builds community,*' I hear George MacLeod saying in the background). Living in a hut on the White Plains of eastern Poland, not far from the border with Russia, we were a mixed bag of trainee theologians: Baptists, Orthodox, Presbyterians, Catholics and Methodists, all in our 20s. Over the evening campfire, talk turned to belief, theology and eventually to baptism. And in the heat of the flames, and conversation, I found myself arguing my line of thought fiercely. In a lull, I realised I was arguing for a concept about which I really knew very little. I was taking time to push my line, rather than to learn about my friends' *'experience of the Light'*. That was a turning point for me, after which I realised that to live out my passion for unity I had to be prepared to set aside my own beliefs for a while in order to hear those of others.

In Place for Hope (www.placeforhope.org.uk) we support people of faith, many in local churches, as they transform conflict and embrace difference. Working with groups, we initially agree ways to ensure that our gathering will be effective. These are agreements to which we will hold one another in the course of our work. They can act as a steady rock while all else may seem fluid. One of these agreements is that we will listen to 'one voice at a time'. This means that when one person is speaking, others listen. Full attention is given to the speaker. This also means 'stilling the voice in our head'. There may be no one else speaking, but the voice in our head may be rehearsing a response, a reaction, a refute to what has been said.

- *As we search for peace and (comm)unity in the church, are we prepared to sit lightly to what we hold dear in order to understand more fully the Light of the other?*

- *In our search for unity among believers, to what extent are we looking for community, or for uniformity?*

5. Peace in the world

'Bring into God's light those emotions, attitudes and prejudices in yourself which lie at the root of destructive conflict, acknowledging your need for forgiveness and grace. In what ways are you involved in the work of reconciliation between individuals, groups and nations?'

(Advices & Queries 32. *See also 33, 34, 35, 36 and 42*)

The Truth and Reconciliation Commissions of Rwanda, Northern Ireland, Liberia and South Africa remind us that many great hearts and minds have, over decades, worked tirelessly for reconciliation through attentive listening, forgiveness and the grace of God. The Forgiveness Project (http://theforgivenessproject.com), Forgiveness Challenge (www.forgivenesschallenge.com), and the Elders (Mary Robinson, Desmond Tutu, Kofi Annan and others: http://theelders.org) remind us that many great people are still putting their energies into this task of peace and reconciliation.

We can all be agents of change, or 'global elders', in the sense that we are, each one of us, called by God to be peacemakers in the world.

In the Quaker tradition, an elder is someone who is *'responsible for fostering the spiritual life of the meeting'*. In other traditions, elders are *'men and women called and committed to ... help release, realise and enrich the full Christian potential implicit in the spiritual calling of all those in the Church and, indeed, in the wider society they encounter in everyday life'.*[23]

- *In what ways are you a global elder in your own community?*

- *What does forgiveness mean to you? Share a story of a powerful experience of either giving or receiving forgiveness.*

The call to Love: Sermon for Sunday, 17th April 2005 (John)

(Scripture readings: Exodus 13:20–22; 1 Thessalonians 5:9–11; John 13:31–35)

'Just as I have loved you, you also should love one another' (John 13:34b, NRSV). This must surely be one of the best-known sayings of Jesus. It is certainly the saying that gets right to the heart of what it means to be a Christian disciple. The world judges us by how well, or how badly, we live up to this commandment. It is the standard we know we are asked to live by.

How ironic, therefore, that in John's Gospel this core commandment of Jesus is bracketed by betrayal. Immediately before he speaks, we see Judas slinking out into the night, to betray him to the religious authorities. And immediately after Jesus speaks, we hear Peter making his vow of loyalty – *'I will lay down my life for you'* – a promise which, we know with sad certainty, he will almost immediately break.

But it is surely no accident that John brackets this saying with the harsh reality of betrayal. For is it not the case that, from the very moment when he spoke these words – *'love one another, as I have loved you'* – Jesus' disciples have betrayed him, have let him down?

A moment's reflection on our own experience surely confirms this for each one of us. If I were to pick out one example, among many, where I know I failed to love my fellow disciples as Jesus loved me, it would have to be the time, many years ago, when I was sent by the Iona Community to lead a small team of people at the Abbey on Iona. Iona, that small island off the West Coast of Scotland, attracts thousands each year to its rebuilt medieval Abbey. Our Community is responsible, in partnership with Historic Environment Scotland, for the Abbey, and for offering hospitality to all who come. When I was sent there, I know now, looking back, that I went with very fixed ideas of how we should do things. I was so sure of the validity of my ideas, that I completely failed to recognise the validity of the different ideas of the team that was already there. In essence I loved my own ideas more than I was prepared to love the people I was sent to lead. I did not, in truth, love them as Jesus loved me.

As we read this Gospel passage, therefore, we not only hear, and want to respond to, this high command of Jesus. We also hear, and recognise within ourselves, the betrayal of Judas and the broken vows of Peter.

But the good news is that this honest, if painful, recognition need not end in despair. The children of Israel, wandering in the desert of Sinai on their escape from slavery in Egypt, were no strangers to betrayal and broken vows. The story of the Exodus is littered with accounts of failure and backsliding, as the freed Hebrew slaves grumble and complain and disobey on their tortuous journey to the Promised Land. And yet, here in our reading from the thirteenth chapter of the book of Exodus, we see God promising to lead them along the way with a pillar of cloud by day and a pillar of fire by night.

Our God is an utterly trustworthy and reliable guide. Our calling is to be his travelling people, and to put our trust in him. God knows we will betray him, and break our promises as we go. Such is his mercy and grace, however, that he does not walk away – he stays, reliable and trustworthy, and keeps on showing us the way to go.

But we must keep on moving. As individuals, and as churches, we must keep on moving. It is when we stand still, out of complacency or obstinacy or fear, that things start to go wrong. In the Iona Community, we have a saying – *'follow the light you see, and pray for more light'*. I often use this picture to help people grasp the importance of keeping on moving. I ask – as I ask you now – to imagine yourself standing just inside the door of a strange room. You have never been in this room before, and it is completely dark. All you have for light is a small candle, which you are holding in your hand. You have to walk across this room to the other side, where there is another door for you to leave. You know, because you have been told, that the room is full of furniture. You hold the candle up high, trying to see the furniture, so that you can avoid bumping into it. But if you remain standing where you are, just inside the door, you will never see far across the room – and eventually the candle will burn out, and then you really will be in the dark. So the only way you will get across the room is if you take a risk and start moving – and of course, as you move, the candle moves with you, and lights up the furniture bit by bit … until you safely reach the other side.

Trust in God, and keep moving! As individuals, growing in the faith – leaving behind old fears and fantasies, laying down old sins and habits, even letting go of past successes as well as past failures – always moving on. And as churches too – letting go of past history, of traditions that served well once but no longer match the needs of today – always moving on. Our God is trustworthy and reliable, despite all our betrayals and broken promises – he will lead us forward, if we keep moving on.

And as we journey, St Paul tells us, we are to encourage one another and build each other up. For we are called, are we not, into community? Today, at least in the world of northern and western Europe, community is hugely at risk. From every side, we are under pressure to live fragmented lives. Isolated in our nuclear families, driving around in our individual cars, struggling to keep our short-term jobs, coping with our consumer society, beset by a culture centred on instant gratification, it is harder and harder, is it not, to feel part of any meaningful community today?

How vital, then, that the church should celebrate our calling into community. For God does not intend us to be disciples on our own. The whole story of salvation is about God's calling us into community: from God's first covenant with the children of Israel to Jesus' gathering of his first disciples into the community of the new covenant, the church.

And as we celebrate God's calling us into community, of course, we also recognise how we need community, if we are to be disciples today. For we cannot do it on our own. We're not talking here simply of the warm fellowship of the local congregation. Community is more than fellowship. Another saying the Iona Community has is *'a demanding common task alone can build community'*. It is surely as we take on together the demanding common tasks – praying together, sharing our money, tackling huge and complex social problems, working at supporting the vulnerable in our midst, struggling to protect the environment, to name but a few – that we will find ourselves truly in community.

And so we go on. A travelling people, always on the move – for the church is a movement before ever it is an institution. But a travelling people with a reliable guide – God, in Christ, always going on ahead of us, showing us the way. And a community of travelling people – committed to the demanding common tasks, and supporting and encouraging each other on the way. Yes, each one of us has within us a bit of Judas, and a bit of Peter. But like Peter, and even like Judas, it is to us also that the Risen Christ still turns, with love and forgiveness in his eyes, and looks on us with clarity and with hope, and says to us, as he said to them: *'Just as I have loved you, you also should love one another. By this everyone will know that you are my disciples, if you have love for one another.'* (John 13:34–35, NRSV)

Holy Week and Easter

Introduction (John and Ruth)

One Holy Week on Iona, in the early 1970s, the Warden of the Iona Community's Centre in Glasgow brought up a group of homeless men he knew to stay in the Abbey for the week. These were men living on the very edge of society, extremely vulnerable and needy. Their walk through that Holy Week with those of us who formed the Resident Group at the time was a truly memorable experience.

For a start, as we sought to enter together into the struggles of the first disciples, as they tried to make sense of what was happening in their lives, we were brought face to face with the very real struggles of the men from Glasgow, trying similarly to make sense of the lives they had to live day by day. For their part, as they told us, it was a strange and affecting experience to be invited into our community, to experience what has been called the 'radical hospitality' of the Iona Community.

To move with them, from the struggles of Holy Week to the harsh reality of the Crucifixion, and then followed by the great celebration of Easter, was to move yet again into mystery. In one sense, of course, there was little mystery about the Crucifixion. You could see it coming a mile off. Yet in another sense, the Crucifixion confronts us with two levels of reality and two sorts of mystery. On the one hand, we see Jesus being willing to die for the love of these few dozen men and women – as also for these homeless men and for us in the Resident Group – while at the same time giving his life as a means of making eternally and utterly substantially real the depth of God's love for the whole of God's creation.

The story of Holy Week and Easter mirrors the story of our lives, of all life – solid, often harsh, reality combined with awe-inspiring mystery.

Living in inner-city slums in Glasgow in the middle of the 20th century, John had to work alongside very damaged young adults who could see little good for themselves as they looked ahead in their lives. One evening, in despair at his struggle to maintain meaningful relationships with them, he complained to a senior colleague: 'In all honesty, I really don't like these kids, and I know they don't really like me.' The reply, when it came, sounds almost pious when read out of context – but it made sense eventually. 'You don't have to like them. Your job is to love them.' And the reality of that, which was also a bit of a mystery, was the requirement to stay close to them, to walk with them as much as possible on their hard journey, and to never give up on them. As this same senior colleague wrote, in a note found in a drawer in his house after his death, about a young man he had accompanied through thick and thin, a very damaged young man indeed: 'I have known that he is very mixed up, but have decided to proceed on the basis of refusal to reject, no matter how foul.' Reality, and mystery, all mixed up together.

The mystery and the reality continues. Holy Saturday, an intrinsic part of the Easter story, is a time of not knowing. A day to be allowed its uncertain, unknowing place in the narrative. It warns us of the danger of allowing Good Friday reflections to propel us too quickly into the known, into the reality and the mystery of Easter Day. Ruth remembers a Good Friday sermon where the preacher moved, within the space of 10 minutes, from a reflection on the destructive power of the cross, to a celebration of the Resurrection. Both part of the Easter narrative, but the gallop through the story denied the space to lament, to grieve, to wait in the not-knowing.

That first Saturday was for the early disciples, a day of disaster and despair – the essential element, of course, in any journey to hope and new life. The experience of both of us, in Interim Ministry for the Church of Scotland and in working through conflict and change with Place for Hope, has shown us that the need to experience and own our brokenness is essential for any healing process to take place. Just as Jesus was the protagonist in the first Easter story, so is it not true that we are called to be the protagonists in our own stories of reality and mystery, entering as fully as we can into the experience of sorrow, grief, lamentation and waiting, before we can ever expect to move on to hope and new life?

On Iona, people have been able to symbolise this journey through the shared travelling through Holy Week. They identify with the key characters in the story, share the Passover meal, strip the church and clothe everything left in black. And then go on to share the awe-inspiring experience of midnight in the darkened church as Easter Day begins. Then, on Easter Morning, they gather in the Relig Odhrain, the Abbey graveyard, to celebrate the Good News that 'Christ is Risen, Risen indeed.'

Nor does it always have to be an experience restricted to the sacred buildings. Ruth remembers vividly Easter 1983. Watching the sun rise over Ben More in Mull on Easter morning from the top of Dun I, Iona's highest hill. Running with a group of friends to St Columba's Bay on the southern edge of the island to celebrate the sacrament of baptism in the sea. Then running back to the Abbey, picking daffodils on the way to decorate the Easter cross for the procession along the Street of the Dead into the church, where the resurrection story comes alive in the sharing of bread and wine – serving the elements in welly boots and woolly jumpers. Thoroughly exhausted, yet thoroughly alive. Living the story of the Risen Christ in body and soul, with others for whom going to church wasn't the goal – but living the story most certainly was!

Holy Week reflections (John)

The following reflections were first shared with the congregation of Canonmills Baptist Church in Edinburgh during Holy Week of 1997. Each evening, and also on Easter Sunday morning and on Easter Monday, we gathered in their small building, once the schoolroom where Robert Louis Stevenson was a pupil, and took time to reflect on the events of each day, based on the scripture readings for the day.

Monday: The scent of love

Scripture: John 12:1–7

The writer of the fourth Gospel has given us here one of the most beautiful stories of Holy Week – and also one of the most skilfully constructed.

Let's think for a moment about what he has actually done.

First of all, he has taken three quite separate stories that were obviously in common currency among the little Christian communities of first-century Palestine, and woven them into one. There's the story, clearly mentioned in verse 1, of the raising of Lazarus. There's the story of Martha and Mary and the dinner party they gave for Jesus, found in another place entirely, in the Gospel of Luke. And then there's the story of the woman who poured expensive perfume on Jesus' feet and wiped them with her hair: a woman described in another Gospel simply as *'a sinner'*, but here, in John, named as Mary, Martha's sister, the hostess at the meal.

Then there is the rich symbolism of this skilful story, as John tells it. It's six days before the Passover: to Jewish readers, the number six, one short of the perfect number seven, would signify the incompleteness of this event, but would also suggest that things were coming to a climax – as indeed they were.

Setting the story in the home of Lazarus, the man Jesus raised from the dead, points with dramatic urgency to the course that events are about to take in a few days' time, underlining the power of God already at work in this Man from Galilee. The half-litre of perfume – a pound in weight, in old money! – was expensive indeed: more than a year's wages, on Judas' estimate, for an agricultural worker of the day. For Mary, as far as we know simply an average housewife, this was a gift of quite extraordinary generosity.

And finally, John's comment that *'the sweet smell of perfume filled the house'* stands in stark contrast to his words in the previous chapter, when Martha warns Jesus that if he raises Lazarus from the tomb, there will be a very bad smell indeed. John here, it seems, is doing everything in his power to prepare his readers for the events that are about to unfold: his comment about the wretched Judas, that he was *'a thief'*, reminds us that before we get to the denouement, we will have to face some pretty desperate times.

Now let's try to enter personally into these dramatic events – dramatic and provocative, as Jesus seems deliberately to dare the religious authorities to do their worst.

How strange, that in the midst of such an escalating drama, that we are invited to watch him enter, with apparent ease and unconcern, into the domestic intimacy of a family home. And how almost bizarre that in this haven of peace and friendship, in the middle of an increasingly hostile and threatening situation, that we see this beautiful interchange – an interchange, effectively, of personal, and utterly vulnerable, love.

We are so accustomed to the great central statement of the Christian faith, the love of God for all people, demonstrated by the willingness of Jesus to go to his death for us all, that we can forget, if we are not careful, that Jesus didn't just die for all people – he died for the love of very specific individuals, starting perhaps with Mary here, and continuing right up to ... each one of us here: for the love of you and you and you ... for the love of me.

His love led him to the cross for individuals, with individual names and stories. Whenever I am in danger of forgetting that, I think of Jim (not his real name). Jim came to Iona when we worked there in the 1970s. He worked in the Abbey as a volunteer for six weeks during his summer holidays from college. While he was there, he shared something of his family history. His parents had separated; his father was an alcoholic, and since his father had left home, they had lost touch with him. Jim had heard that he was living rough in London, and before he left Iona he told us he was hoping to go there, to see if he could find him.

Months passed. And then at the beginning of November, Jim phoned. He had gone to London; had spent long days and nights searching for his father; and had eventually found him, living in terrible conditions. And to cut a long story short, he was phoning to ask if he could bring him up to Iona with him for a few days at Christmas.

Well, they came, the two of them, and stayed until after Christmas. His dad was in a very bad way, and a recent stroke had seriously impaired both speech and movement. He was desperately grateful to his son for searching him out, very conscious as he now was of the wreck of a father he had become.

Shortly after they left, Jim phoned again. On returning home, he had taken his father to his mother's house, where he had had a further stroke, and was now more or less completely incapacitated. His mother, moved to pity, had agreed to let him stay, and was now nursing him in the family home. When Jim phoned again, it was to tell us that his dad had died; and he shared with us the peace and reconciliation that he and the family had found at the end.

Love, just ordinary and yet so extraordinary human love, is

surely nothing if it is not personal, and vulnerable, and costly. And if that is true of human love, with all the mixture of altruism and selfishness that is in all of us – as I think that story of Jim and his dad so wonderfully illustrates – then how much more true must it be of the love of God. Here at the start of this week, which has an effect quite simply cosmic in its significance, we see a demonstration of the personal, costly, vulnerable love of God in Christ, which is so much part and parcel of its continuing attraction, and significance, still today.

Unless, of course, we think, like Judas, that love can be weighed, and measured, and doled out according to a strict code of morality and pragmatic righteousness ... and only to the deserving poor ...

Tuesday: The challenge to religion

Scripture: Mark 11:15–19

You may know the film of St Matthew's Gospel made many years ago by the Italian Communist film director, Pasolini. He made it in black-and-white, using amateur actors; and for me, one of the most powerful scenes is this very one, the cleansing of the temple.

The actor playing Jesus is a young man, of course, as Jesus was – thin, and very pale-faced. As he plays it, you get the strong impression that he is interpreting Jesus' emotions as a mixture of anger and fear; he literally jerks and stumbles his way around the courtyard, his body movements so tense and stiff that you can't help but feel the tension in your own body, in your own heart.

My sense is that that was most probably the way it was for Jesus, at that moment. For this wasn't just any old religious building – this was the building at the very heart of both the Jewish faith and the Jewish state: and it is a desperately dangerous thing to do, is it not, to challenge religion when it is bound up, and backed up, with the power of the state?

For a period in the 1990s my work took me, on a number of occasions, to Croatia, a part, of course, of the former Communist Republic of Yugoslavia. And there I have seen, and I have heard of, some of the terrible things done in our time, in the heart of our continent of Europe, by religion and the state combined. It's not just the buildings – the demolished mosques and the destroyed and desecrated Catholic and Orthodox churches, all viciously attacked in the name of religion and the state – that bear witness to this frightening combination when it goes wrong. Much more, it's the damaged souls and spirits of the people, in whom these three expressions of faith in a just, loving and merciful God have turned sour and bitter, sowing the seeds for a future harvest of hatred, perhaps over many generations. Thank God there are, in the midst of this, many wonderful, gifted, committed and brave individuals, of all three faiths, working constantly to counter this hatred with costly acts of service and love.

So what is the challenge that Jesus – the Jesus of the cleansing of the temple, the young, scared, brave and angry Jesus – poses to religion, now, in our day?

It's too simple, I think, to suggest, as has been suggested, that Jesus' challenge to religion was that he wanted it done away with. Living as we do in times which have witnessed many terrible religious abuses, and also in a society like ours where now only a minority of our fellow citizens practise a live religious faith, it might be tempting to think that Jesus wanted religion done away with. But that is not the evidence of scripture. His own custom was to practise the religion of his ancestors, the religion of first-century Judaism; he prayed, he attended the synagogue *'as his custom was'*, he knew the scriptures, he loved the religious traditions of his people. Furthermore, all the evidence, even of our own irreligious age, points to the fact that men and women today continue, perhaps paradoxically, to believe in God, to seek *'that of the Spirit'* somehow in their lives.

Nor can we honestly say that the influence of religion, in particular of the Christian religion, is all bad. In a lecture, Dr Garret FitzGerald, former Taoiseach of the Republic of Ireland, argues, with some force, that the Christian ethos and principles of Europe, developed over nearly 2000 years – and despite all the failures – have been the main factors in four intellectual revolutions that have helped to change the course of history in the second half of the 20th century. He names these as, firstly, the emergence, through the Council of Europe, of the concept of personal human rights that transcends the sovereignty of the state; the idea, in other words, that countries like Serbia can no longer protect their criminal politicians, who abuse their fellow citizens, from the full force of international law.

A second revolution is the emergence, through the European Community, of a profound rejection of war as an instrument of policy; who now, he asks, can imagine any major European nation-state deciding that it is acceptable to pursue policy by going to war with its neighbours?

A third revolution is the abandonment by Europe of colonialism, at least in its more blatant forms, and the acceptance of the principle that the rich should aid the poor, rather than exploit them – although the international debt crisis is still a huge mountain to climb.

And fourthly, he identifies the important growth in recent times in ecological consciousness through the Green movement, which, he says, has created a new moral imperative on a global level.

These four fundamental shifts, as he calls them, in political thought in the second half of this century have emanated from Europe and would, he argues, appear to derive largely from the

Christian ethos as it developed over the centuries in this continent. And we may add that, within and through this same Christian ethos were, and still are, millions of faithful Christian men and women, practising their faith much as Jesus did – saying their prayers, attending services, reading the Bible and loving the traditions of their ancestors. Is it not through such ordinary faithfulness that the world is changed?

What, then, of the challenge that Jesus is posing to religion? Yes, he was angry – frightened too – as he cleansed the temple. But we need to remind ourselves that when he came to the Mount of Olives and looked down on Jerusalem, we are told that he didn't look at the Holy City with cold eyes and a bitter heart – instead, he wept.

It seems the challenge that Jesus posed, and always poses, to religion is that it has to be a force, not for dogmatism or captivity, but rather for freedom, a force for kindness, a force for good. Yes, the very word 'religion' comes from the Latin for 'to bind'. But any binding that religion does has surely to be to the God whom Jesus knew – the God he called 'Father' – and to the kingdom of that God which Jesus, by his words and his whole life, showed us was within each one of us. Ours is not simply a religion of stories, however hallowed, powerful and meaningful they may be; it is first and last a religion of 'salvation' – a word whose root meaning is '*to set in a wide open space*'. If we receive it, and practise it, with that understanding always in mind, then, with God's help, it can surely always be a force for good in our lives, and in our world.

Wednesday: Choices

Scripture: Matthew 26:14–16

What are our thoughts, our feelings, as we enter, perhaps with some difficulty, into this event of Holy Week – the betrayal by Judas?

Do we go along with the view, which seems certainly to be suggested by the way Matthew tells the story, that Judas betrayed Jesus for cash? That seems an unlikely interpretation, when you remember that Judas estimated, a few days earlier, that the cost of the ointment Mary poured over Jesus' feet came to the equivalent of a whole year's wages for an agricultural labourer, and that thirty pieces of silver was little more than a month's pay. Hardly a sufficient sum, you would think, to be the sole reason for betraying his Master to his certain death.

Much has been made, we know, of the possibility that Judas was a Zealot, the advocates of armed resistance to the occupying Roman forces. If this is true, then it could be argued that Judas had become gradually disillusioned with Jesus' attitude to the political issues of the day; perhaps exemplified by his low-key entry into Jerusalem, on a donkey, on Palm Sunday. Maybe Judas had hoped for a very different sort of Messiah – one who, as many also seemed to hope for, would come to lead an armed uprising, like the Maccabees a few centuries earlier, like other 'Messiahs' who had come and gone before. So possibly his act of betrayal was an attempt to force Jesus' hand; to bounce him out of his commitment to the non-violent way, into a more combative, more aggressive role?

Well, we can speculate on Judas' motives for this act of betrayal – but we can never really know. And the more I reflect on this story, the less I am inclined to want to know why, and the more I am personally challenged by it, and moved, very deeply moved, by Jesus' response.

I am challenged by it. Judas, it seems to me, is not that much different from the other eleven disciples, at least in this respect: he is concerned more with his own agenda than with the agenda of Jesus.

Think for a moment about the whole group of disciples as they move around Jesus during this crisis-laden week. The Gospels concentrate on Judas – for he did something so final, and so terrible in its effect, that it naturally attracts the most attention. But you could argue that the others were not a lot better. On their way up to Jerusalem, what are they doing but arguing among themselves over who is the greatest! Jesus is on his way to his death, and they are concerned about their own status and future honours! And then, a few days later, in the Garden of Gethsemane, after the moving events of the Last Supper and the feet-washing, what do they do but fall asleep – and when the police arrive, after a futile attempt at defending him by only one of them, they all forsake him, and flee! And as if to add insult to injury, while Jesus is being interrogated by the police, what does Peter do, but deny any knowledge of him – not once, not twice, but three times!

When you put it alongside these sad and pathetic examples of so-called 'loyalty', Judas' act of betrayal doesn't seem to me to be all that much worse. Yes, his betrayal had a more immediate and dramatic outcome, but the actions of all of them, Judas' included, did they not grow out of precisely the same condition? All of them, whether they were arguing over honour and status, or falling asleep, or running away, or denying him, or betraying him – all of them, it would seem, were taken up entirely with their own concerns – none of them were seized with the concerns, and the purpose, of Jesus.

And this is surely a challenge to me – for I know I am very much in the same boat as the disciples. I'm not a player of the same stature, of course – nor am I playing on anything approaching the same stage as any of them. But my concern, if I'm honest, is very similar to theirs, most of the time. It's my agenda, rather than the agenda of Jesus. 'Lord, Lord' I may say with great regularity – but how often do I seriously seek to be truly open to the concerns and purposes of the kingdom of God? Judas' story asks me to stop, and think, and seek help from the Spirit, that God may enter my life more deeply than I usually care to allow God to do, so that my concerns may be less those of honour and status and influence, less those of the simplistic solution and the easy option – and much more the kingdom concerns of the Man from Galilee.

And Jesus' response to the betrayal of Judas moves me deeply. At the very least, Jesus must have suspected Judas' intentions; indeed the Gospel account suggests that he actually knew what Judas was going to do. But no word of reproach escapes his lips – he simply lets him go, and when the time for the betrayal arrives, Jesus calls Judas 'my friend' – and accepts his kiss.

On Iona, many years ago, we had a lovely set of six communion cups and plates, made of glass. They had been specially commissioned for the Abbey – and round the lip of each cup was engraved a suitable communion text: 'This is my blood'; 'Drink this, all of you'; 'Do this in memory of me', and so on. When the craftsman, who was not a churchgoer, was asked to make them, he requested that he could be allowed to choose one of these texts. And the text he chose was the question Jesus asked of Judas when he came with the soldiers: 'Friend, wherefore art thou come?'

'Why are you here, my friend?' Jesus asks this not just of Judas – he asks this of me, of us all. No judgement. No accusation. No defence. Jesus simply treats us with great courtesy and great respect, even as we go on with our own agendas and our own concerns – and often, oh so often, at the same time betraying him, again and again.

Is it not a wondrous thing to be treated thus by the One who created us? How will we, with something approaching the same courtesy, the same respect, answer his question? The choice is ours.

Maundy Thursday: Breaking

Scripture: Mark 14:17–31

Such a familiar story, isn't it? We hear it every time the Sacrament of the Lord's Supper is celebrated. I'm not at all suggesting here that its familiarity, as can sometimes happen, breeds contempt – but it is perhaps appropriate once in a while to stand back from the story, and take another look.

We are so used to concentrating on Jesus' actions – the breaking of the bread and the sharing of the cup, the central acts in our Communion liturgies – but what about the context in which he does these things?

For instance, each of the first three Gospel accounts brackets Jesus' actions with intimations of betrayal, of desertion, of denial – in Mark's words, *'one of you will betray me', 'you will all become deserters', 'before the cock crows twice you will deny me three times'.* Matthew and Luke say the same. In John's account, it's even sharper – after Jesus has washed their feet, and Peter has tried to stop him, he tells them *'one of you will betray me'*, he tells Peter *'you will deny me'*, and when he tries to tell them what he is really doing, they say to each other, in their confusion, *'we do not know what he is talking about'.*

What are the Gospel writers trying to say to us here? Rather than inviting us to see this story as a beautiful account of a special and holy meal, I suggest that Matthew, Mark and Luke in particular (and John too, in a more nuanced way) are saying, in effect, that Jesus has reached the end of his tether!

For what has happened? For three solid years these men – and women too – have been constantly in his company. They have heard him preach. They have seen him heal. They have watched him share food with the outcasts of society. They have seen him challenge the religious authorities. They have heard story after story after story about the coming reign of God. Now they have followed him to Jerusalem, the centre of earthly power.

And he looks around at them, sitting there – and what does he see? Fellowship? Support? Understanding? Solidarity? No. He sees betrayal. He sees denial. He sees misunderstanding. He hears disputation – as Luke puts it *'a dispute arose among them as to which one of them was to be regarded as the greatest'*. This is what Jesus sees and hears, from his nearest and dearest, as he approaches the climax of his mission.

And I find myself wondering – in face of what looks like the complete failure of his followers to actually get what he has been on about for these three years – is it too fanciful to imagine that Jesus, having tried everything else to get them to understand, in frustration, in desperation almost, uses the bread and the wine to say, in effect: 'All right, I've got nothing left to offer – take my body, broken for you – it's all I can give you now'?

What about us? In a moment we will share bread and wine. Are we any clearer than these first followers as to what Jesus is really about? As he looks around at us, what does he see and hear today? There's no denying that over the 2000 years that separate us from these events in the Upper Room, there have been many denials, many betrayals, many huge misunderstandings about his mission – both in the church and in the world at large. Do we know, today, what he is talking about?

Perhaps it is to John's account that we must turn – to that more nuanced, more reflective attempt – to help us make sense of Jesus' mission. In the washing of the feet, Jesus' act of unconditional love catches at our throats and at our hearts in a way that nothing else can do. Brian Wren puts it superbly in the third verse of his wonderful hymn, 'Great God, your love has called us here'. With this in mind, can we come to the table now?

'Great God, in Christ you call our name
and then receive us as your own,
not through some merit, right or claim,
but by your gracious love alone.
We strain to glimpse your mercy seat
and find you kneeling at our feet.' [24]

Friday: The day called 'Good'

Scripture: Mark 15:16–39

For whom did Jesus die?

We say – the Church has always said – that he died for all people – and this is surely true. In Christ, says St Paul, there is neither Jew nor Greek, male nor female, slave nor free – all, all are one in Christ. So – Jesus died for all.

Yes – and so, this means, he died for me. This, too, the Church has always believed – and I believe it – believe that he died, not simply for everyone, and certainly not primarily to found yet another religion – but I do believe that he died for me. And this is indeed a most astonishing and wonderful thing – as Paul, again, puts it: *'God proves his love for us in that while we were still sinners Christ died for us'* (Romans 5). That's me.

But that is not enough. That's right – Christ died for all – Christ died for me – but I want to say more. I want, somehow, to say this:

I want to say – Christ died for Alec. For Alec – whom we all knew as Dodger – whom I buried. Alec, dead of a heart attack at 43, after a lifetime battle against his particular addiction, which happened to be the fatal one of alcohol, not so unlike, perhaps, the many different addictions that plague and pester us all at various times in our lives. I want to say that Christ died for Alec – and even as I say it, I feel the weight of the sense of failure of so many of us who loved and cared about Alec, and who saw and experienced the good in him – can we say the Christ in him? – for he was indeed one of the least of these brothers and sisters of his that Jesus spoke about ... remember?

So I want to say that Christ died for Alec. And I want to say that Christ died for Alec's mum, Betty. Betty, who died just before her son, and who spent virtually the whole of the second half of her life in the locked ward of a psychiatric hospital after a life of hardship and struggle in a forgotten and abused part of the great city of Glasgow. I want to say that Christ died for Betty, and again, as I say it, I feel the weight of the sense of the sadness of so many folk who loved Betty, and who saw the gentleness and the goodness in her, despite her awful pain – who saw the Christ in her, shining through.

Yes, and I want to say it, and to say it again and again, till the words numb my pain and dry up my tears, never mind the tears *they* shed and the pain *they* bore – I want to say that Christ died for all these, whom the world may count as nothing – and they counted themselves so often as nothing too – all these who so often in the night-time cry *'would God it were morning'*, and in the morning cry *'would God it were night'*.

For whom did Jesus die? Yes, he died for all; yes, he died for me; yes, he died for ordinary, everyday, good folk whose lives are ordered and whose days are mostly glad. But I can never forget that he was crucified by good religious folk and by the servants of the legally constituted authority of the day – and I never want to forget that the first person to enter paradise after him, he said, was ... a thief.

Holy Saturday: Waiting

Scripture: Mark 15:42–47

I wonder if this day in Holy Week – Holy Saturday – isn't in fact the day of all days in this strange, mysterious week with which most of us – perhaps all of us – can most readily identify.

I ask this simply because I imagine most of us, if not all of us, have experienced what the friends of Jesus – Mary Magdalene, the other Mary, and all the rest – experienced on that first Holy Saturday. I imagine most of us – perhaps all of us – have experienced a bereavement – a family member, a friend, a work colleague – have had to cope with the whole gamut of emotions that bereavement brings. Grief, shock, disbelief, numbness, fear, guilt, anger, physical sickness, pain, sense of loss and total lostness – mixed, hopefully, at some stage with acceptance, a sense of peace – most of us, perhaps all of us, have known something of what the disciples were going through that day. We have been there too.

I remember a week when I was involved with two deaths, two funerals; the one a much loved family doctor and friend who died after a long and positive life; the other a former member of a youth club I once helped to run, his life a constant battle against addiction.

For us all on these occasions, just as for the disciples, memories are so important. Mostly, for me, it's not the 'if only' thoughts that surface after a bereavement – these can come, but later. No, for me, the memories that crowd in immediately are all the good times, all the positive and caring ways of the person who has died. They bring tears, of course, these memories, as I try to come to terms with the hard realisation that these good things are gone now, never to return. But with the tears, I find mostly that they bring some comfort – precisely because these good things were unique, they belonged uniquely to that one person, they are precious, they are special, and they are still mine.

But now, behold, a mystery! For it seems that God does not leave us with these memories stuck in the past tense, stuck in stone, as unchanging and seemingly permanent as the busts and sculptured figures of the dead of which our ancestors seemed so fond. As life gradually returns to something approaching normal, the memories may fade, but the person remains very real – not stuck in the past so much as, can we say, waiting in the wings, as if permanently on tiptoe, expectant, waiting for the cue which might bring them back on stage again?

That cue, and indeed that stage, are of course things over which we have no control – and that lack of control can produce in us widely varying reactions. People can turn to spiritualism, to Ouija boards, to search for that elusive control. Or they can deny that sense of waiting expectancy, and view death as final – the last full-stop, the snuffing out of life's candle, the victory of darkness over light. I suppose some may deal with it by turning in on themselves, wallowing perhaps in guilt, in shame, or even making a bit of a public show of their mourning and their grief.

Or – can we deal with it by standing on tiptoe ourselves, expectant, watching, anticipating some sign, some wisp of a movement which might, just might, transform the whole scene?

For the first disciples, clearly the overwhelming feelings seem to have been ones of total despair – and we can surely feel for them. And for those who look on the earthly life of Jesus and see no more than that, this day must surely be the day when they turn away and say – 'well, he was a good man, or a madman, or something in between – but he's gone now, and we must move on'.

But for we who are within the community of faith – we who now live with the knowledge of what will happen tomorrow – on this Holy Saturday we are invited to stand on tiptoe, expectant, waiting, looking for some sign, some movement, some cue which will transform everything. So let us have the courage to be open to whatever that transformation will bring – to us, for us, for our lives and for the life of the world today, and every day.

A prayer:

God of life,
we have come now,
with the first disciples,
to the place of despair and death.
With them,
we have witnessed
the awful power of hatred,
fear and greed,
working their ways with frail flesh,
and once so fragrant hope.

With them,
we have felt the shock
of iron on bone,
of state power over puny mortals,
of religious righteousness
over the faint freedom of faith.

With them,
we have heard the well-loved voice
fall silent,
seen the deeply loved face go vacant,
the eyes grow dim,
the flesh turn cold.
Death has had its way
with all that they, and we,

held most dear,
in Jesus, the Man from Galilee.

Dear God,
you know
that we have been here before.
Been here,
not just with the first disciples,
but on our own,
watching a loved one die.
We are not
strangers to death,
we know its ways.

Help us now,
on this Holy Saturday,
to hold our hand
from any final action,
to hold our breath
from any final word.

Teach us once again
the truth of our creatureliness:
that we are not the masters of our fate,
nor the captains of our souls.
Keep us open
to your possibilities
now through this watchful night
and in the face of every dying
with which our living is filled
from birth to our final moments;

so that we,
with all the followers of Jesus,

may be able
to be surprised by joy,
in the face of the seeming
finality of death.

We ask this
in the name of this same dead Jesus
in whom the possibilities of God
wait their time.

Amen

Easter Day: Fear transformed

Scripture: Luke 23:54–24:11, John 20:1–21

You've maybe heard the story of the little girl in the Sunday school class, who was found one morning sitting quietly by herself, drawing. 'What are you drawing?' asked her teacher. 'A picture of God,' came the confident reply. 'But nobody knows what God looks like' was the startled response. 'Oh, but they will,' announced the six-year-old, 'when I've finished my picture.'

I imagine we have been trying to draw that picture, as a human race, since time began. People are still at it today. There was the mass suicide in California a while ago of the followers of a cult called Heaven's Gate. They killed themselves, it seemed, because they had come to believe that God was calling them to leave their earthly bodies and to join him in a spaceship which was following in the wake of the Hale-Bopp comet that was in the Earth's skies at the time. Their search for God led them to this extreme action; but there are many millions who are searching for their own picture of God in less extreme ways, with philosophies, with drugs, with bits and pieces of different religions, through spiritualist encounters, and so on – the Internet seems to be stuffed with such theories and suggestions. And, in a way, they are all on the same path as that little girl in the Sunday school – trying to draw their own picture of God.

And some might argue that we Christians are in the same boat – that we too are trying to draw *our* picture of God – that the faith in Jesus' resurrection which we celebrate today is every bit as strange as some of the wilder ideas referred to a moment ago. What are we to say to this charge?

Perhaps, first of all, we can say this. In many of the attempts people make to draw their own picture of God, there seems to be one common element: namely, that to find God, human beings must somehow escape from the limitations, the complexities, the ambiguities of life on earth. Escape is the watchword – escape either by wild theories or by promoting a few stark certainties – from the constant struggle of having to be fully human. The older theologians described this as trying to escape from 'the flesh'.

This is a common temptation. In dramatic style, of course, the Gospels showed Jesus facing exactly the same temptation. Turn stones into bread – and escape from the constant human struggle for food. Jump unharmed from the top of a high mountain – and force the astounded onlookers to acknowledge that we are not the weak and vulnerable human beings that we really are. We may even have tried to use the power of religious conviction to escape from the trap of the flesh and the ambiguities of this world – many have tried to do exactly that.

But if we have truly walked with Jesus over these past days of Holy Week, then I believe we can truly say that he has shown us another way.

For is it not the case that, in Jesus, God has shown us that, in that fully human life, far from seeing the world and the flesh as some sort of trap from which we have to escape, God has become embedded in the world and the flesh, not in order for us to escape from them, or to show us a way out of them, so much as to show us how to fully accept them, and to let God transform them?

So we have seen Jesus transforming the meaning of greatness – showing us that true greatness is to serve, that true greatness is to be found in deep humility: the donkey-riding, feet-washing God.

We have seen Jesus transforming the meaning of love – showing that true love, tough love, is vulnerable and costly and personal – never weighing and measuring its price.

We have seen Jesus transforming the meaning of religion – showing us that true religion is about liberation, not captivity – liberation into committed, disciplined action for the values of God's reign in this world – mercy, justice, humility.

We have seen Jesus transforming the meaning of leadership – sharing, not imposing, working from below, not deciding from on high.

We have seen Jesus transforming the meaning of suffering – showing us that through suffering, accepted and carried in all the weakness and brokenness of its awful weight, with courage and with love, and even when it is totally undeserved, there lies the possibility of new life.

I suggest that this is, in part, our answer to the charge that we Christians are just another escapist sect. In Jesus, we claim to have seen God engaged with our fully human life at its deepest and at its most costly – and, thus engaged, transforming it for us all. And we all know what sort of a response is asked of us – to engage ourselves, in turn, with God's help, in all that makes for human living – and so to seek to be agents of God's transformation in the here and now.

But there is one more question which, on this day of all days, is rightly asked of we who claim that God raised Jesus from the dead. For on this day of all days we are rightly asked – and what do you say about death?

Here, I must ask you to allow me to give my personal testimony – for theologies, creeds, formulas and dogmas, in the face of the stark witness of the Gospel accounts we heard a moment ago, stumble, and fall.

I do not know what exactly the first disciples experienced on that first day, that turned them from a bunch of frightened cowards into the courageous apostles of the faith. All my life, I have had to accept the possibility that they were deluded, that it was all in their minds, that they made it all up.

But every time I go back to the story, in all honesty I cannot say that what they experienced, however mysterious, was anything other than absolutely and completely … real.

And for myself? Well, I have met no Jewish Rabbi of the first century AD. I have heard no heavenly voice, touched no nail-torn hands, put my fingers in no spear-pierced side. But day after day I have experienced the reality of a Jesus who is no dead legend, but a living, transforming, challenging presence in my life and in the lives of others around me. His is the transforming presence that shoves me, often against my cautious nature, to take action, however small, for justice and peace. His are the words that illuminate the confusing verbiage that pours over me every day. His is the healing, enabling power that picks me up when I would at times gladly lie down, and … yes, escape!

And finally, it is the transforming mystery of Jesus' resurrection that I trust, when I look death – of my loved ones, of my friends, of myself – in the face. For what I see and what I hear is not the crashing shut of the door of life, and the smothering blackness of the eternal dark; what I see and hear is the interchange between a woman called Mary and the Man she mistook for the gardener. 'Jesus said to her, "Mary" – and Mary turned to him and said, "My teacher!".'

So – what does God look like? Ask rather, who is God like?

God is, we confess, like Jesus, called the Christ. And Christ is Risen … He is Risen indeed!

Easter Evening: Stories

Scripture: Luke 24:13–35

When you come to think about it, what was actually happening on the road to Emmaus was, at one level, simply the telling of tales.

Here were the two disciples. Walking along, they were, I guess, doing what we've just been doing: telling each other the stories of the past few days, and of their lives. Telling the stories, too, of their hopes and expectations as members of the people of Israel: *'We had hoped he would be the one who was going to set Israel free!'*

And they were telling, as well, the story of the mystery of that first Easter Day: *'Some of the women of our group surprised us; they went at dawn to the tomb, but could not find the body.'*

They were telling, then, the stories that gave their lives meaning, the stories that pointed to their hopes as a people, the stories that hinted at the possibilities of a new faith. They were telling their stories.

Left to themselves, their stories were only leading, however, to despair. Then, into their company, comes Jesus. Jesus, whom they do not know at first; Jesus, who listens carefully to their stories, their tales. Jesus, who then tells his stories. Or, to put it another way, Jesus who takes them through their stories again, and reinterprets them, so that their stories come to be seen in the light of his story, and so become, not stories leading to despair, but rather stories leading to hope.

And when it comes to evening, and the breaking of bread – suddenly they know Jesus in their midst, and things click, things become clear, and their stories now make sense in the light of his story, and *'wasn't it like a fire burning in us when he talked to us on the road and explained the scriptures to us?'*

Can it be that what we need to do, most urgently, and most constantly, is to seek to put ourselves in exactly the same relationship to the Risen Christ as that of these two disciples on the Emmaus road?

As individuals, as families, do we not need to tell our stories to Christ, and ask him to reinterpret them back to us through his story? Our loving – our struggling – our doubting – our winning and our losing – all the questions and answers that define and delineate our rich, chaotic, wonderful, confusing, gloriously ordinary human lives – these stories, do we not need constantly to be telling them to the Risen Christ – and then listening hard as he tells them back to us through his stories, as we have them in the Gospels, to his stories as we hear them in our hearts? So that our stories become, not stories in danger of leading to cynicism and despair, but rather stories leading to new hope?

And do we not also need to be doing this as part of the church, the body of Christ in the world? Especially today, when things are changing so fast, and we may be in danger of telling ourselves only the stories we feel comfortable with – stories of how it was in 'the old days', stories of how it might be if 'the old days' would only return? Do we not need rather to tell the whole stories of the hopes and expectations of the church – of a world renewed, of justice established, of true peace which is, in the wonderful words of a modern meditation by Brian Wren:

'... *the shouting of children at play,*
the babble of tongues set free,
the thunder of dancing feet,
and a father's voice singing.'?[25]

Are these not the stories we need to be telling each other, in the Church – and telling them in the presence of the Risen Christ, only to hear him reinterpret them, for us, in the light of his own story, over and over again?

It has been truly said that we live out of our stories. We have heard again, this Holy Week, the central stories of our faith. I believe God asks us now to set our stories and these stories side by side. I believe God asks now, and every day, to let the stories of our lives, and the stories of our church – yes, and the stories of our nation too – be permeated with the stories of the Risen Christ, crucified, risen, ascended and promised to come again. Only thus, can we be moved out from our safe shelter. Only thus, can we be motivated for courageous action in the world. Only thus, can we truly witness to the resurrection faith. And only thus, as our stories merge with Jesus' story, and become transformed, will it then surely come to pass, in the words of Desmond Tutu, that it will be true that:

'...*Goodness is stronger than evil;*
love is stronger than hate;
light is stronger than darkness;
life is stronger than death;
victory is ours, through Him who loves us.'[26]

Easter Monday: Through wood and nails

Reading: John 21:1–14

We look out on a very different world today from the world of first-century Palestine. In present-day Palestine it's a world of tension, of fear, of hatred – gun-toting Jewish settlers and stone-throwing Palestinians, faltering peace talks amidst suicide bombs in cafés and bulldozers violating ancient Palestinian vineyards and orchards.

And in present-day Britain? A world of ... what? All the ills that flesh is heir to, the rise and fall of public figures and football teams, the traffic, the weather, the markets, what's on the telly, who's coming to dinner, what will the next century bring?

Well, this is our world, a chancy, changing, yet familiar world, the one we have been given to live in, not chosen, but it's ours, and we will never live in another.

And out into this world we are asked to go, to love it and to serve it in Christ's name. How may we do this?

I used to think, in my youthful arrogance, that we were to go out rather like 19th-century missionaries sailing off to 'darkest Africa'. We had Christ – we were to bear Christ to the unbelieving world – we were to tell of Christ as we understood him, no matter who or what stood in our way – and if we were persecuted, or even if we failed, then that only proved that we were 'doing the Lord's will'.

I don't see things so simply now. This story especially, of the disciples meeting the Risen Christ in their daily work, made me revise my views, for a start. I know now that our calling is to be faithful in our ordinary daily tasks – in the home and the shop and the workplace and the street – there, I now see, is where we are to witness to the Risen Christ.

For, of course, that is where the Risen Christ already is. This story shows me, above all, that I was mistaken to imagine that it was I who was going to carry Christ to others. Christ is already there, waiting for us all to recognise him. An American theologian has put it well: '*We do not carry the Gospel to others; we mutually exchange the life that Christ has revealed to us all.*' And I am reminded of the way our Celtic forebears in the faith saw things: setting up what St Columba called their 'colonies of heaven' in the midst of the ordinary lives of their neighbours, witnessing as much by their lives as by their words to the presence of the Risen

Christ, already there before ever they came. And wasn't it St Francis who sent his brothers out into the turbulent world of medieval Europe with the exhortation: *'Go, and preach the Gospel – using words only when absolutely necessary!'* Teilhard de Chardin, the great French scientist and Jesuit scholar, wrote:

> *'What men cannot hear because of the feebleness of my voice, what they shut their ears against so as not to hear it, this I can confide to Christ who will one day tell it again, to their hearts.'*[27]

Finally, I'm reminded by this story in the Gospel, that it all comes down, in the end, to love. Perhaps, as the disciples pulled in their bulging nets, felt their muscles ripple and rejoiced in their strength, they were tempted to believe that there was now nothing that they could not achieve. Perhaps, as they sat beside Jesus on the lakeshore, eating and drinking with him, they were tempted to believe that all who saw them would now be bound to believe too, and join their band.

But then, of course, Jesus takes Peter aside, and asks him, three times, 'Do you love me?' Gives him three chances to negate the three denials in the courtyard, three days ago, before the cock crew. And so brings him, and the others too – and you, and me – right back down to earth with a bump. Right back down to where Jesus was – and had always been – and will always be – and is here now – the vulnerable, serving, suffering, disciplined, committed, sensitive, caring, dying, and always loving Jesus – inviting Peter, and the others – and you and me – not so much to worship him as to follow him, in loving God and our neighbour, and ourselves – and leaving all the rest … to him.

Theologies of transformation for Holy Week (Ruth)

There is a deep need for peaceful transformation of dispute, conflict, war and violence in our world. As Christian believers we are guided by a teacher committed to active non-violence; our Christian story is rooted in a toolkit for transformation, hope and radical reformation.

I offer here brief reflections from the spiritual root that gave birth to Place for Hope: the Christian story of life, death and new life, as focused in the particularity of the Easter story. This story is couched in three movements, or 'times'.

Time for lamentation: Good Friday

Beginning with Good Friday, the day on which Jesus is tortured and crucified, we are reminded that there is a time for lamentation. In the confusion and pain of the Crucifixion, there is a time to acknowledge trauma, hurt, woundedness, fear, pain, grief. Our faith story is rooted in having the *courage* to walk towards sorrow both as grief-stricken participant and as empathic observer. A root element in our faith is that awful trauma happens, that God may seem absent (but is not), and that people get hurt, and even die. We are invited to move towards pain, through fear, into bewilderment, hurt and grief. This is part of our faith story. In times of conflict and danger, when disintegration seems close, a human instinct says to avoid danger and potential pain. Sometimes this is not possible. We have a model and a precedent in the Good Friday story of lamentation.

Time for not knowing: Holy Saturday

Moving towards Holy Saturday, we know there is a time for not knowing: a time of limbo, of heightened fear and uncertainty, of pondering, reflecting, wondering – time for reflection, for coming together, for learning with one another, for building resilience, for looking for support, for not rushing towards the answers, for the courage to wait. *The Stature of Waiting*, by W.H. Vanstone, and *Grain in Winter*, by Donald Eadie, powerfully bear witness to the resilience of being a Saturday people.

For the disciples this waiting time lasted for three days. For others this time of not knowing, in the midst of grief and pain, may last much longer; if we are caught up in a lengthy dispute, or in a grief that seems interminable, this time may seem never-ending. Waiting in this time of not knowing also means being able to discern when to stop waiting. Because waiting doesn't mean stalling, but means active, discerned waiting – having the courage to know when to act.

Time, and a place, for hope: Easter Sunday

Finally, we are Easter people. Unlike the disciples, we do indeed live in the knowledge of the Resurrection. Easter Sunday and the Resurrection reveals to us that there is a time, and a place, for hope. Not a wishful-thinking hope that if we bury our heads in the sand, the world's, and our own, problems will go away. But a cosmic hope that through the pain and the waiting there is a possibility of totally human and utterly cosmic transformation – both mysterious and deeply ordinary at the same time.

As the mystery of birth is both miraculous and commonplace, so the mystery of death is both miraculous and commonplace – and the choice we have is to move towards pain, and possible death (metaphorical or real), with courage, with patience and with hope.

By exploring the rich faith traditions into which we are born and within which we can grow, we discover wisdom for the journey towards reconciliation, and so open the door to a clutch of theologies of reconciliation.

Prayers for Easter Day (John)

Easter prayer 1

Risen, glorious Christ,
we join with all your people
in heaven and on earth
to greet you
and to celebrate once again
the great victory you have won!

And what a victory!

Beneath you, defeated,
lie all humanity's ancient foes:
pride, self-sufficiency, status,
security, even death itself.
By your triumph on the Cross
you have put in their proper place
all we have come to rely on
for life itself:
friends, health, family,
occupation, achievement, success.
Lifted high on the Cross,
you hold up before us
the ultimate power of love:
Risen glorious from the tomb,
you stand beside us now,
our brother, our servant,
and the living God.
What can we do
but worship,

and praise,
and seek again to follow?

Master, for us, you know full well
the strife is not o'er,
nor is the battle done.
And even as we celebrate
the completeness of your triumph,
still and still we need to seek
strength and succour
for our lesser struggles,
day by day.

Please forgive us if,
in our warfare
against all that would dehumanise
and defile creation
and our fellow creatures in it,
we forget your way
of waging battle,
and fail to use your weapons,
those weapons of truth,
of unconditional love,
of faith and hope
and complete trust in God.

Hear us, and help us.
We pray in your name. Amen

7th April, 2002

Easter prayer 2

Glory be to you,
God, our strength and our redeemer.

The vacant cross
and the empty tomb
vindicate your claim
that the love which suffers
is the love which saves.

Fill your people then with joy
and your church with celebration
that the world may know
that your holy son Jesus
is not a dead hero we commemorate
but the living Lord we worship –
to whom with you and the Spirit,
one God,
be all glory and praise
now and for ever.

Lord Jesus,
here are some of your disciples –
your wounded hands and feet
in today's world.

At times we have been the frightened ones
keeping our distance,
worried about our safety
or our reputations.
But you come close to us
bringing peace and challenge,
unlocking our potential,
setting us free.

At times we have been the confused ones
feeling far from you
with questions that have no answers.
So help us now
as we listen to what you have to say.

The Risen Christ says:
'Peace be with you:
as the Father sent me,
so I am sending you.'

So send us now, Lord –
through our fear,
through our doubt,
through our confusion –
that we may continue
to do your work
as we travel our many roads,
liberated and united by your resurrected love.

We pray in your name. Amen

22nd April, 2001

Easter prayer 3

At the start of the story of the liberation of the Children of Israel
from slavery, God says to Moses: 'My Name is I AM.'

At the start of Jesus' Passion, and the story of our liberation from
sin, guilt and death, when the soldiers in the garden ask Jesus if
he is the one they have come to arrest, he too says: 'I AM.'

We come into the presence of the God of
the Present Tense, of the Present Moment,

of the Now: so let us, now, worship Him.

Present – at the beginning of all things:
creating – rejoicing – loving everything
into being:
Present – in the story of a people –
liberating, agonising, suffering, seeking:
Present – in the story of Jesus –
healing, sharing, dying, rising,
promised to return:
Present – in the story of the Church –
comforting, disturbing, challenging,
empowering:
Present – in the life of the world –
hidden – hoping – waiting – watching:
God of the Present Tense, hear us,
and help us, now.

And if we have thought to turn you
into Past Tense –
if we have thought of you
and talked of you
as yesterday's God
for yesterday's Church
in yesterday's world –
then forgive us, we pray.

If we have thought to turn you
into the Past Tense –
believing that your power and your love
are no longer available today,
and we just have to get on without you –
then forgive us, we pray.

And if we have tried to push you
into the Future Tense –
thought of you as for other people
and for other times –
perhaps even mainly for
after we are dead –
then forgive us, we pray.

Spirit of the Living God,
present with us now,
liberate us from any captivity
to the past,
and any anxiety about
the future.

Firm in our faith,
and in the company of the faithful
who have gone before us,
who surround us and uphold us
here and now,
may we live this day and every day
in the presence of the One
whose name is always
'I AM.'

We pray in Jesus' name. Amen

25th April, 2004, Canonmills Baptist Church, Edinburgh

Easter prayer 4

We thought we had heard it all,
dear God; we thought we knew.
The Bible stories;
the words of our faith;
the rules for living
and the way to heaven;
we thought, dear God, we knew!
But here,
before the mystery again
of a grave that is empty
when it should have been filled
with a decaying corpse,
we know now
that we know nothing at all.
Lord, have mercy on us!

We thought we had heard it all,
dear God; we thought we knew.
The great stories of the church;
the ebb and flow of the faith;
our place in the scheme of things;
we thought, dear God, we knew!
But here,
before the mystery again
of death defeated,
of broken folk made whole,
and mighty powers quite broken,
we know now
that we know nothing at all.
Lord, have mercy on us!

We thought we had heard it all,
dear God; we thought we knew!
The way of the world;
the powers that be and
the powers that would be;
the ebb and flow of armies
and international finance;
the endless tide of refugees
and the awfulness of hate;
we thought, dear God, we knew!
But here,
before the mystery again
of a word of love
in a quiet garden,
and the promise, suddenly,
of a new order of creation
in place of the old, tired, familiar scene,
we know now
that we know nothing at all.
Lord, have mercy on us.

Easter prayer 5

Risen Christ, we greet you!
Every power on earth and in heaven
had thought to consign you to the grave.
Politics and religion, avarice and jealousy,
cowardice, confusion and fear –
all had conspired to bury you,
all had thought – half afraid – that they'd won.
But God was faithful;
God honoured your life

by raising you from death,
so that even the shattered disciples could say:
'Christ is Risen! He is Risen indeed!'

Risen Christ, we greet you!
How often have we, in our day,
thought to consign you to the grave!
Half afraid, how often have we thought
to bury your way of tough love,
of sacrifice, forgiveness, peace;
to turn away from your call
to live in responsible freedom
in our complex, changing world.

Christ, have mercy.
Lord, have mercy.
Christ, have mercy.

But God is faithful still;
still God honours your life
within and among us,
forgiving and renewing, so that even we can say:
'Christ is Risen! He is Risen indeed!'

Risen Christ, be with us now.
Not just here, at your table (in this service)
gathered and renewed as your faithful people.
Be with us, in home and shop,
office, workplace, school and street,
so that, in all our living,
day by day, graced by your Spirit,
we may proclaim, with lip and life:
'Christ is Risen! He is Risen indeed!'

Ascension and Pentecost

Introduction (John and Ruth)

If Christmas is about incarnation and mystery, if Lent is about humanity and the reality of struggle and conflict, if Holy Week and Easter are a journey through the reality of despair to the mystery of hope and new life, then Pentecost and Ascension are surely about an opening out – a thrusting into the wideness of the whole world. This season is an affirmation of spiritual experience much wider than Christianity, embracing those of Judaism, of Islam, of Buddhism, of Hinduism, of secularism. It is a true throwing wide of the gates. It was the late great Ian M. Fraser who reminded us that the word for 'salvation' in the Bible comes from a root word that means 'space'. Salvation is an opening out to life in all its fullness, never a closing down into some dogmatic or exclusive position.

In the Book of Acts, the first Pentecost is all about the bursting of the Good News out of its original Jewish context into the who of the then known world. '*We are from Parthia, Media and Elam; from Mesopotamia, Judaea and Cappadocia; from Pontus and Asia; from Phrygia and Pamphlyia; from Egypt and the regions of Libya near Cyrenia. Some of us are from Rome, both Jews and Gentiles converted to Judaism, and some of us are from Crete and Arabia – yet all of us hear them speaking in our own languages about the great things that God has done!*' (Acts 2:9–11). Pentecost and Ascension are *still* about the opening up of the Good News of God's love in and through Jesus Christ to the whole world, to the *oikoumene*. This is a truly ecumenical gift that God seeks to give to all people everywhere, on whichever faith journey they find themselves.

What does this gift of true openness ask of us today? It surely asks us to know ourselves so fully embedded in the very best of our own faith tradition that we are able to let go of it, in order to see and embrace 'the other' authentically. Ruth found herself confronted with just that demand as a student in an ecumenical work camp in Poland, when she realised that she had to let go of her own beliefs in order for them to be reinforced and remoulded by the beliefs of others. She became aware of the need for deep listening, in order to be able to suspend her own beliefs for a while – as John Paul Lederach says, in the context of conflict trans-formation, we need to suspend our assumptions, our story, '*from the ceiling*',[28] in order truly to embrace 'the other'.

There are undoubtedly huge challenges in being this open. In our community life on Iona, we make big demands on ourselves, on our staff and our volunteers. We ask them all that we be open to the hundreds of 'others' who come to stay with us all the time. Sometimes that can be at the expense of giving ourselves time and space to explore, first of all, who we ourselves most fully are – although that knowledge can creep up on us precisely as we do open ourselves to others. And we must always recognise, and put in place to manage, the danger of burnout, of anxiety and stress on an unacceptable scale.

Jesus calls us '*to be one*'. This is not a call to an amalgam, to a lowest common denominator sort of oneness. Rather, it is a call to the wholeness of humanity, to the risky business of accounting to ourselves for our beliefs and practices, so that we '*choose life*' in the sense of allowing ourselves to go on a trajectory of widening out from a place of profound self-acceptance. To do the opposite – to go on a journey that takes us to a place of solidifying, of setting in stone, of always looking back and 'turning into salt' – that is to choose, not life, but death.

Reflections on Spirituality (John)

George MacLeod, founder of the Iona Community, once wrote that *'there are few words more dangerous than "spiritual"'*. I don't have the original context in which that sentence appeared, so I don't know exactly what he meant by it. But certainly for much of my life I had a fairly fundamental suspicion of the word, and its accompanying noun 'spirituality'. I felt uncomfortable with the connotations of 'other-worldliness' and 'airy-fairy-ness' that they carried; and in my defence, they are, are they not, often used with that meaning in mind?

Then I came across this passage, in the book *Free at Last?*, by the American Orthodox writer Jim Forest:

> *'Dukhovnost … literally the word means "quality of spirit" … while referring to the intimate life of prayer, also suggests moral capacity, courage, wisdom, mercy, social responsibility, a readiness to forgive, a way of life centred on love … it means all that happens in your life when God is the central point of reference.'*[29]

That thought – that 'spirituality' is about everything in your life when God is *'the central point of reference'* – is echoed, I think, at least to some extent, in one of Evelyn Underhill's comments, when she writes that *'a spiritual life is simply a life in which all we do comes from the centre, where we are anchored in God: a life soaked through and through by a sense of His reality and claim, and self-given to the great movement of His will.'*[30]

This insight, that 'spirituality' is not something 'other-worldly' and 'airy-fairy', but in fact is to do with the whole of your life, was very releasing for me at the time – very empowering. However, at that point I was still thinking of it solely in religious terms, as expressing how one's whole life could be defined in relation to God being at the centre. Which is fair enough, so far as it goes.

Then the next word of wisdom that came my way on this matter was from Kathy Galloway, who offered what I think is a very helpful definition of spirituality as *'that which ultimately moves you – the fundamental motivation of your life'*. And suddenly it came to me that really, just as everyone has a 'materiality', so everyone has a 'spirituality'; the issue is what is made of them both throughout one's life.

Thus, in relation to our common 'materiality', we can either honour and care for our bodies and our possessions in a generally responsible way – echoing St Paul's appeal to the Christian community in Rome to *'present your bodies as a living sacrifice, holy and acceptable to God'* (and interestingly, he adds here *'which is your spiritual worship'*!) or, of course, we can abuse our bodies and our possessions, through neglect, through drink and drugs, and so forth.

The same, I sense, is true about our common 'spirituality'. If Kathy is right, and spirituality is indeed the ultimate motivation in our lives, then it can be honoured – and indeed honoured by offering it, and thus our whole lives, to God – or it can be abused. For can we not say that the 'spirituality' of the Nazis in the 1930s and '40s – that which ultimately motivated them, and of course then led to all the horrors of that period – was their hatred of the Jews and their conviction of the superiority of the so-called Aryan race? Was that not their 'spirituality', just as the apartheid system was the 'spirituality' of many of the white South Africans throughout the last century – just as, we can perhaps say, greed and the profit motive is the 'spirituality' of many in our society here in the West today?

In this way, I found myself feeling able at last to release my understanding of 'spirituality' from its imprisonment in the chiefly religious field, and set it free to relate in reality to the whole of our lives; and it is the whole of our lives, both the material and the spiritual, that surely needs to be converted, through and through, day by day, by the only Spirit that has the power to do that – the Holy Spirit of God.

Having said all that, what I'm still trying to understand is the way that so many people in our secular, consumerist culture are seeking spirituality without any reference whatsoever to God, or even the 'transcendent'. People talk of a 'spiritual deficit' in our society, but don't necessarily thank you if you suggest that religion (or, heaven forfend, the Church!) might be a place to look to deal with this. I think I can understand where many such folk are coming from – mostly from a place where religion, or the church, has either never been present, or has been present in a very un-attractive style. And when I listen to them, they are often using words and phrases which I readily associate with 'spirituality' – words like 'values', 'generosity', 'justice', 'solidarity with people living in poverty', 'peacemaking', and so on. What I often find missing, though, are two things. On the one hand, any underlying narrative, or set of myths, which underpins their sense of 'spirituality'; and on the other hand, a community which holds them together, and holds them to account, for their living out of these values. People may often come together, for instance, round a single issue, and find in that *demanding common task* a real community of purpose; but when that issue goes, or they move on, what then? Is it not all very fragmented and individualistic? Or is that just the way it is anyway in today's Western society? And what does this say to the Church, to the way we do things, with our age-old narratives, our structures which are so cumbersome and hier-archical, our style of worship with its emphasis on 'telling' rather than 'dialogue', and our embeddedness in the establishment?

Prayers for Ascension and Pentecost (John)

A prayer for Ascension Day

Let us give thanks
for all the signs of the Lordship of Jesus
in our world today.

For Christian men and women
offering themselves for election to public office;
for those who serve Christ
in the civil service
and other fields of public service;
for all who seek to walk Christ's way
in the world of business, commerce and industry;
for those who seek to honour Jesus
in the caring professions;
they seek to honour Christ;
we would honour them.

For congregations working quietly
to welcome refugees and asylum seekers;
for men and women of faith
struggling to overcome the debts of nations
in order to feed the nations' starving people
and to home the nations' homeless ones;
for Christian teachers, parents, youth workers,
celebrating the kingdom amongst the young;
for old people, and their carers,
facing the end of one stage of the journey,

approaching in faith the next;
they seek to honour Christ;
we would honour them.

Prayer for Pentecost

Spirit of God,
flickering over our heads,
illuminating our faces,
inspiring our thoughts,
give us now, we pray,
words of joy and praise.

Spirit of God,
filling our hearts with hope,
steadying our nerves with peace,
comforting our lives with love,
give us now, we pray,
words of joy and praise.

Spirit of God, come to us now –
surging through the darknesses
of our lives –
sweeping over our wearinesses;
that in this time of Pentecost,
the sparkling light of faith,
the rushing wind of hope,
the joyful sound of praise
may echo round the world,
may echo in the church,
and find their response in us.
Give us words of joy and praise,
Spirit of God, we pray.

Affirmation for Pentecost

We believe in a loving God,
whose word sustains our lives
and the work of our hands in the world.

God is life.

We believe in God's Son amongst us,
sowing the seed of life's renewal.
He lived with the poor
to show the meaning of love.

Jesus Christ is Lord.

We believe in the Holy Spirit of Life,
making us one with God,
renewing our strength with Her own.

The Spirit is love.

Prayer for Pentecost

Loving God,
you come among us
in so many different ways.

We look around
and see your hand
in creation –
in the soaring sky,
the restless sea,
the growing earth,
the blossoming trees –
and we praise you, Creating God.

We look at Jesus
and see your hand
in salvation –
humility before arrogance,
love in the face of hatred,
forgiveness in the face of prejudice,
resurrection out of suffering and death –
and we praise you, Saving God.

Today especially
we look at the gift
of the Holy Spirit
and see your hand
at the very centre of our lives –
prompting conscience,
disturbing complacency,
energising action,
commanding involvement,
banishing fear –
and we praise you, very Breath of God.

In a quiet moment now,
we sit in the presence
of God, One and Three,
around us in creation,
before us in salvation,
within us in our very breath –
and give thanks.

Loving God,
you know how we struggle
as we seek to live the life of faith.

Doubts assail us –
are you truly the Creator,
does Jesus really save,
is the Holy Spirit actually within?

Within ourselves
we know anxiety,
faithlessness,
stumbling time and again.

In the confusion of our lives,
we ask:
forgive us when we stumble,
pick us up when we fall,
strengthen and encourage us to try again.

Gracious Spirit,
today we would be joyful –
for you come very near to us now.
Teach us the truth of the saying
that while we can never go back to our beginnings,
and make a brand-new start,
we can, each one of us,
from today, with your help,
move forward, yet again
towards a brand-new end.

We pray in Jesus' name.

Amen

19th May, 2002, Pentecost

Prayer for Pentecost

Dust ...
tiny particles of dust,
offensive to the house-proud,
enemy of the allergic –
and yet from such dust,
you brought forth Life, great God!

Chemicals ...
with strange-sounding names,
alone or mixed together,
analysed and utilised
by scientists and schoolchildren –
and yet from such chemicals,
at your command, came Life!

And yet ...
without your Word,
without your Spirit,
without your Breath,
there would be no persons,
no consciousness,
no mortals, a little lower than the angels!
And so we praise you,
for Life,
and the very stuff of Life,
so wonderfully and intricately made.

Above all,
we praise you
for the gift of human Life,
men and women and children,

made in your image,
made to be your co-workers
in caring for your creation.

God,
forgive us,
for we have sinned.
Made for fellowship with you
in caring for creation
instead we have sought to own it,
we have abused it,
we have betrayed your trust.

And so, because of us,
species die
oceans are polluted,
the air is poisoned,
the ozone layer is pierced,
and we rape the planet
for our own selfish ends.

Given freewill
we have used it irresponsibly
for our own greed,
rather than our neighbours' need;
we have brought chaos
out of the order you created.

For the sake of Jesus,
who came to restore
fullness of life
to the whole created order,
we ask forgiveness,

we seek your mercy,
we look to be made whole again,
that we may work again
for the wholeness of your creation.

How great is your name,
God,
through all the earth!

You are a God of mercy and justice –
in Jesus you have revealed
the fullness of your love for us –
and we are so grateful.

Bless us now, we pray,
with your Spirit within and between,
as we seek to offer you
the worship of our lives.
We pray in Jesus' name. Amen

20th May, 2001

Pentecost prayer

Walls of brick and stone,
roads of metal,
houses, shops, streets –
all the stuff of our common life
dissolving around us now
as we know ourselves
drawn into the community
of worship and praise.

By grace alone,
we are one now

with the church on earth and in heaven,
affirming your glory,
acknowledging our need,
celebrating our belonging
to your redeemed community
in time and in eternity.

Walls of brick and stone,
roads of metal,
houses, shops and streets –
all the stuff of our common life
shimmering and dancing around us now
we know them to be
the places of your presence,
living God.

With eyes of faith
we see you all around us –
know you in our neighbours,
hear you in our homes,
join you in the struggle for justice,
acknowledge your Lordship
in this locality of our daily living.

Walls of brick and stone,
roads of metal,
houses, shops and streets –
forgive us, God,
where we have failed in care.

We hold up to you now
all this stuff of our common life,
and seek your forgiveness
for our failure in stewardship.

God, Creator, Son and Spirit,
God before all time,
God in the midst of time,
God who will still be
when all time comes to an end:
meet us here,
forgive us here,
renew us here,
and bless us with your presence,
here and wherever we go.

We pray in Jesus' name. Amen

21st May, 2006, Gorbals

Concluding words (John and Ruth)

The journey towards this book began as a birthday gift. For her 50th birthday Ruth asked not for material gifts from her family, but for gifts of time and experiences. The gifts that flowed included, among other things, time with John to talk about those deep stories of our shared spiritual journey.

It has been a privilege to spend time in each other's company around the kitchen table and in a chilly Glasgow study to share at such a level. For us it has been a profound experience, for it has been in the sharing of these stories that we have given ourselves the greatest gift of all: the gift of continual growth in faith as human beings. This journey for us is an ongoing one. We hope in sharing a part of this story, it may encourage others on a similar journey of shared gifts and faith.

Biographies

John Harvey is a retired minister of the Church of Scotland, living in Glasgow. He served as a parish minister in Glasgow and Stirling, and as an Interim Minister in Greenock, Edinburgh and West Kilbride. With his wife, Molly, he was a member of the experimental Gorbals Group Ministry in Glasgow (1963-71), and served as Warden of Iona Abbey (1971-76). He also worked in lay ecumenical formation with the Craighead Institute in the UK and in Eastern Europe from 1995 to 2000. He has been a member of the Iona Community since 1964, and served as Leader from 1988-95. He has contributed to a number of Wild Goose Publications; and his Kerr Lectures in Glasgow University were published in 1987 under the title *Bridging the Gap: Has the Church Failed the Poor?*, St Andrew Press (now published by Wild Goose).

Ruth Harvey served, from 2012, as a member of the team running Place for Hope, a Scottish charity accompanying churches and faith communities through times of challenge, change and conflict. In June 2020, she took up the post of Leader of the Iona Community, of which she has been a member since 1993. She has had previous stints of working for the Iona Community, as Editor of *Coracle*, and at all the islands Centres, has written for Wild Goose Publications, and fell in love over kayaks and banoffi pie at the Camas Centre. She is a mediation Practitioner, an ordained minister in the Church of Scotland and a Quaker. She has worked, since 1983, in the field of international, ecumenical spiritual formation with the World Student Christian Federation, Churches Together in Britain and Ireland and various parts of the world church.

ʃourCeʃ and aCknowledgementʃ

1. From 'The Tarn and the Rosary' in *Hawkfall and Other Stories*, George Mackay Brown, first published by The Hogarth Press, 1974, and also published by Triad/Panther Books, London, 1983, and by Polygon, 2004.

2. Elie Wiesel quote, original source unknown

3. 'Tell all the truth but tell it slant', by Emily Dickinson, from *THE POEMS OF EMILY DICKINSON: READING EDITION*, edited by Ralph W. Franklin, Cambridge, Mass.:The Belknap Press of Harvard University Press, Copyright © 1998, 1999 by the President and Fellows of Harvard College. Copyright © 1951, 1955 by the President and Fellows of Harvard College. Copyright © renewed 1979, 1983 by the President and Fellows of Harvard College. Copyright © 1914, 1918, 1919, 1924, 1929, 1930, 1932, 1935, 1937, 1942 by Martha Dickinson Bianchi. Copyright © 1952, 1957, 1958, 1963, 1965 by Mary L. Hampson.

4. 'How long, O Lord?', from *Heaven Shall Not Wait* (Wild Goose Publications, 1987), and *When Grief is Raw* (Wild Goose Publications, 1996). Words: John L. Bell (b.1949) and Graham Maule (1958-2019) copyright © WGRG, c/o Iona Community, Glasgow, Scotland. Reproduced by permission. www.wildgoose.scot

5.'Hear me, Lord, and draw near', from *Psalms of Patience, Protest and Praise* (Wild Goose Publications, 1993), and *Love From Below* (Wild Goose Publications, 1989). Words: John L. Bell (b.1949) copyright © WGRG, c/o Iona Community, Glasgow, Scotland. Reproduced by permission. www.wildgoose.scot

6. From *Encounter with Silence: Reflections from the Quaker Tradition*, John Punshon, Friends United Press, 1987, p.7. Used by permission of Friends United Press

7. From *The Spiritual Life, Evelyn Underhill*, Hodder & Stoughton, 1937, pp.131-132

8. 'Disclosure', from *Watching for the Kingfisher,* is © Ann Lewin 2009. Published by Canterbury Press. Used by permission. rights@hymnsam.co.uk

9. Ron Ferguson quote from his column in *The Herald*, 19.12.02

10. Dietrich Bonhoeffer, original source unknown. Quoted in *Iona Abbey Worship Book*

11. Quote from Richard Rohr, from one of his daily reflections in 2012

12. 'Birth meditation and prayers' – original material taken from *Pray Now, Word of Life*. Used by kind permission of the Church of Scotland. Copyright © Resourcing Worship Team, Mission & Discipleship Council, Church of Scotland 2017

13. From *The New Man: Christianity and Man's Coming of Age*, Gregor Smith, SCM Press, 1956 (The Alexander Love Lectures, 1955)

14. From *The Revelations of Divine Love*, Julian of Norwich

15. Jim Wallis quote, paraphrase of Hebrews 11:1. Widely published on the Internet

16. From *The Rise of Christian Conscience: The Emergence of a Dramatic Renewal Movement in the Church Today*, Jim Wallis, Harper & Row, 1987, and elsewhere

17. 'Praying through conflict' – original material taken from *Pray Now, Word of Life*. Used by kind permission of the Church of Scotland. Copyright © Resourcing Worship Team, Mission & Discipleship Council, Church of Scotland 2017

18. From *Reconcile: Conflict Transformation for Ordinary Christians*, John Paul Lederach, Herald Press, 2014. Used by permission of MennoMedia and Herald Press

19. 'Meditations and prayers for unity in the midst of pain' first published by Churches Together in Britain and Ireland. Used with permission.

20. Paraphrased from the hymn 'We lay our broken world' © Anna Briggs

21. From *Advices & Queries* (The Yearly Meeting of the Religious Society of Friends (Quakers) in Britain), The Society of Friends

22. Inspired by 'A Round Table Church', by Chuck Lathrop, in *Seasons with the Spirit*, Ruth Harvey (Ed.), CTBI Publications

23. From *The Eldership Past and Present*, the Eldership Working Party of the Church of Scotland, 2003

24. Third verse from the text of 'Great God, your love has called us here' (Brian Wren, born 1936), © 1975, 1995 Stainer & Bell Ltd, 23 Gruneisen Road, London N3 IDZ, England, www.stainer.co.uk. Used by permission from 'Piece Together Praise' (Stainer & Bell, 1996). All rights reserved. Also used with the permission of Hope Publishing

25. Quotation from the second verse of 'Say "No" to peace' (Brian Wren, born 1936), © 1986 Stainer & Bell Ltd, 23 Gruneisen Road, London N3 IDZ, England, www.stainer.co.uk. Used by permission from 'Piece Together Praise' (Stainer & Bell, 1996). All rights reserved. Also used with the permission of Hope Publishing

26. 'Goodness is stronger than evil (Victory is ours)', text only, by Desmond Tutu, from *An African Prayer Book*, published by Doubleday. Copyright © 1995 by Desmond Tutu. Used with permission of Desmond Tutu. All rights reserved.

27. From *Hymn of the Universe*, Pierre Teilhard de Chardin, Harper & Row, 1961, p.122

28. From *The Moral Imagination: The Art and Soul of Building Peace*, John Paul Lederach, Oxford University Press, 2005

29. See *Free at Last?: The Impact of Perestroika on Religious Life in the Soviet Union*, Jim Forest, Crossroad Publishing Company, 1990; *Religion in the New Russia: The Impact of Perestroika on the Varieties of Religious Life in the Soviet Union*, Jim Forest, Crossroad Publishing Company, 1990

30. From *The Spiritual Life*, Evelyn Underhill, Hodder & Stoughton, 1937, p.30

Wild Goose Publications, the publishing house of the Iona Community established in the Celtic Christian tradition of Saint Columba, produces books, e-books, CDs and digital downloads on:

- holistic spirituality
- social justice
- political and peace issues
- healing
- innovative approaches to worship
- song in worship, including the work of the Wild Goose Resource Group
- material for meditation and reflection

For more information:

Wild Goose Publications
The Iona Community
21 Carlton Court, Glasgow, G5 9JP, UK

Tel. +44 (0)141 429 7281
e-mail: admin@ionabooks.com

or visit our website at
www.ionabooks.com
for details of all our products and online sales